First paperback edition August 2023

ISBN (paperback): 978-1-954041-22-6
ISBN (hardback): 978-1-954041-20-2
ISBN (ebookback): 978-1-954041-21-9

Published by Creative Sound Press
www.creativesoundpress.com
publishing@creativesoundpress.com

creativesoundpress.com

Playing with Sound

A Sound Books Anthology

Charlene A. Ryan

For Matthew, Aiden, Audrey Anna, and Amelia Claire.

May you always make time to play.

Introduction: How to Use This Book

This anthology comprises the first six Sound Books in their entirety. It is designed for educators in preparation for creative work with students of all ages. Each Sound Book was conceived as an aesthetic visual exploration of sound and the elements of music, while purposefully stepping away from traditional ways of representing sound on paper. The six books are presented in the order that I feel is most progressive in terms of concept complexity, with more easily digestible ideas presented earlier in the book and more complex ones later on. Pitch is explored first, in *Up and Down Sounds*, followed by dynamics, in *Big and Small Sounds*, form, in *Sections of Sound*, texture, in *Layers of Sound*, meter, in *Grouping Sound*, and finally a combination of beat, rhythm, and meter in *Moving Sound*. As a collection of individual books, the anthology is not intended for use with children, although there is no real reason why it could not be, if used as intended with child-adult interaction so that each book is engaged with on its own and concepts are not conflated across books. In a classroom setting this anthology would best serve as a teacher guide, alongside the individual concept-specific books, which are recommended for use with children. The instructions for each book follow a similar line, but it is important to read each one as you begin to engage with a new element of music. Each set of instructions provides details about how to think about and use the images for the specific element being explored. These ideas should be thought of as merely starting points. Individual teachers, parents, and children may have new and creative ways of using the material. Feel free to drop me a note and share your approaches, strategies, and perspectives. I would love to hear from you!

Charlene

CONTENTS

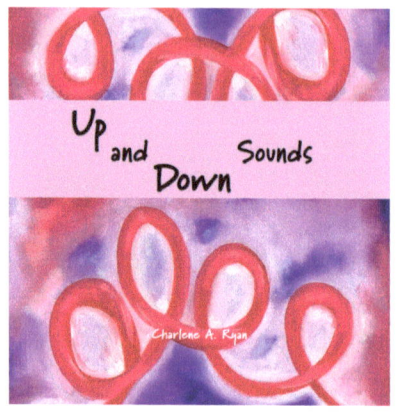

UP AND DOWN SOUNDS....2

BIG AND SMALL SOUNDS....28

SECTIONS OF SOUND....54

LAYERS OF SOUND....80

GROUPING SOUND....106

MOVING SOUND....132

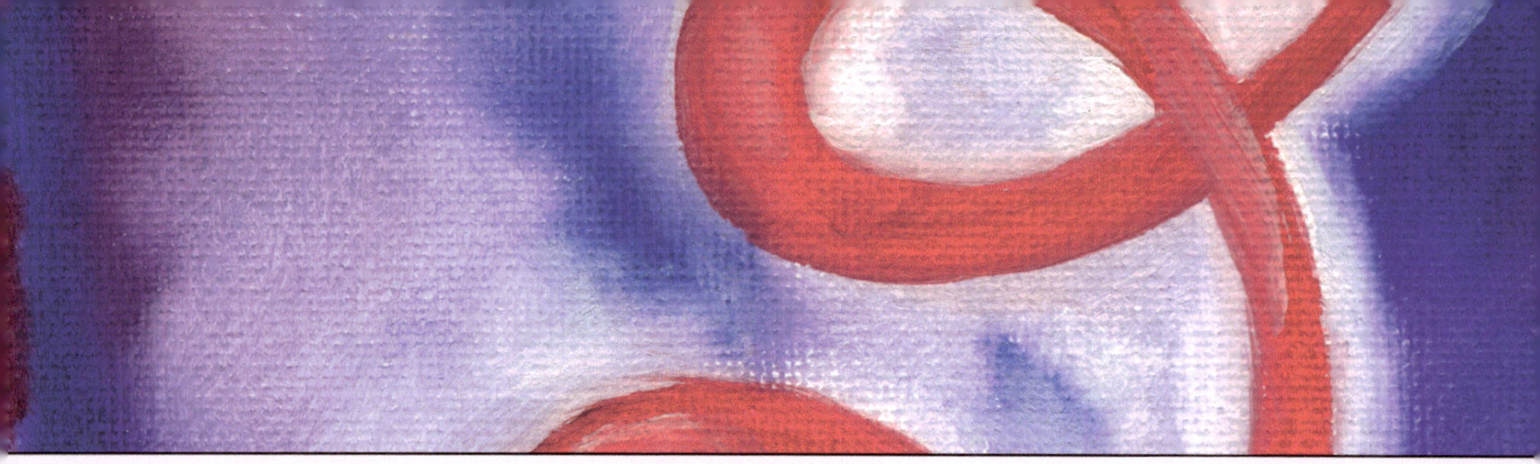

Up and Down Sounds

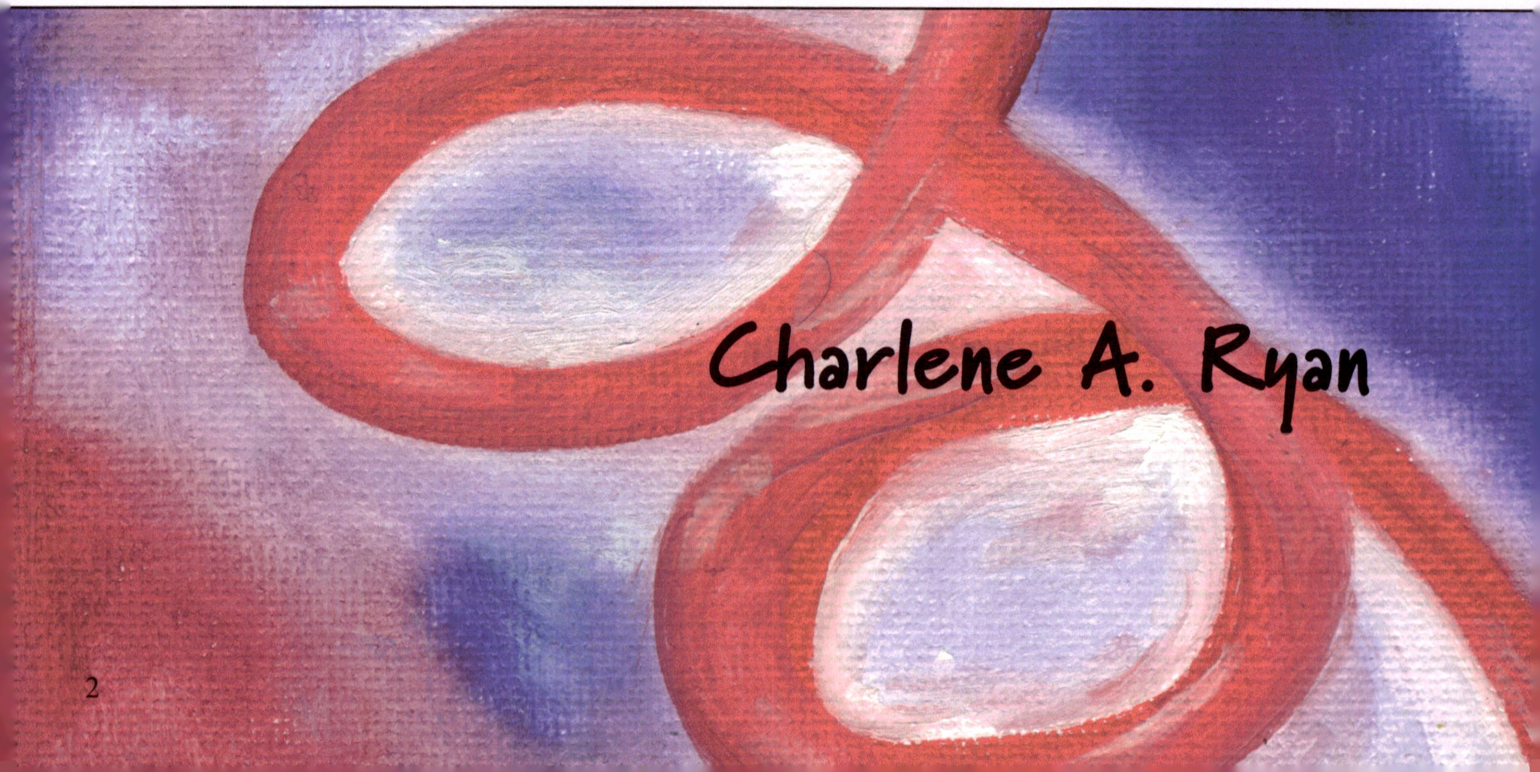

Charlene A. Ryan

How to use this book

Each page is a unique work of art designed to represent higher and lower sounds. The images at the beginning of the book rise and fall in seemingly random arrangements. As the book progresses, so do the shapes, which begin to ressemble those found in traditional musical notation. The artwork provides an aesthetic impetus for engaging children in vocal exploration and forms the building blocks for reading music notation. Encourage children to imagine the sounds that they hear in the images and to think about how the sounds within a given piece of artwork might differ from each other. Ask them to consider what vocal sounds they could use to sing the patterns – oohs, aahs, vums, las, dahs, and loos (and any other syllables they want to try!). And when you've exhausted the book's possibilities, have the children create their own artwork to sing, consolidating their conceptual understanding of pitch and notation, their developing singing skills, and their aural and visual creativity.

Climb the track higher...

and then go down...

Go over the bump...

and now the hump...

Go round and round...

and up then down...

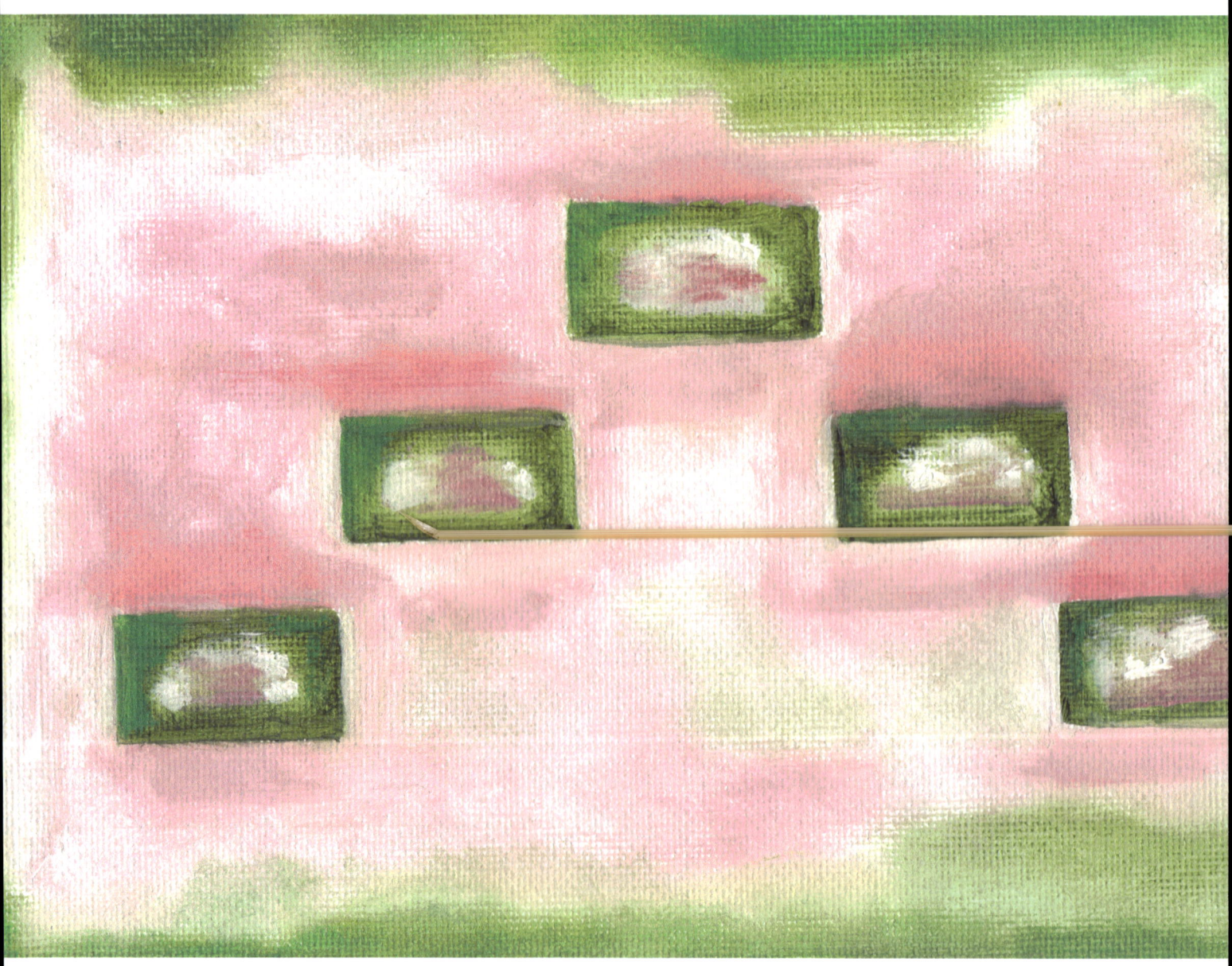

and hold it some...

Now roll and roll...

over hills and knolls...

Smoothly flow...

then loop de loop...

Glide high then low...

16

Which way to go?

Floating higher...

Leap up, then lower...

Far apart…

Close together...

Double the middle...

Leap up, step a little...

Repeat the bottom...

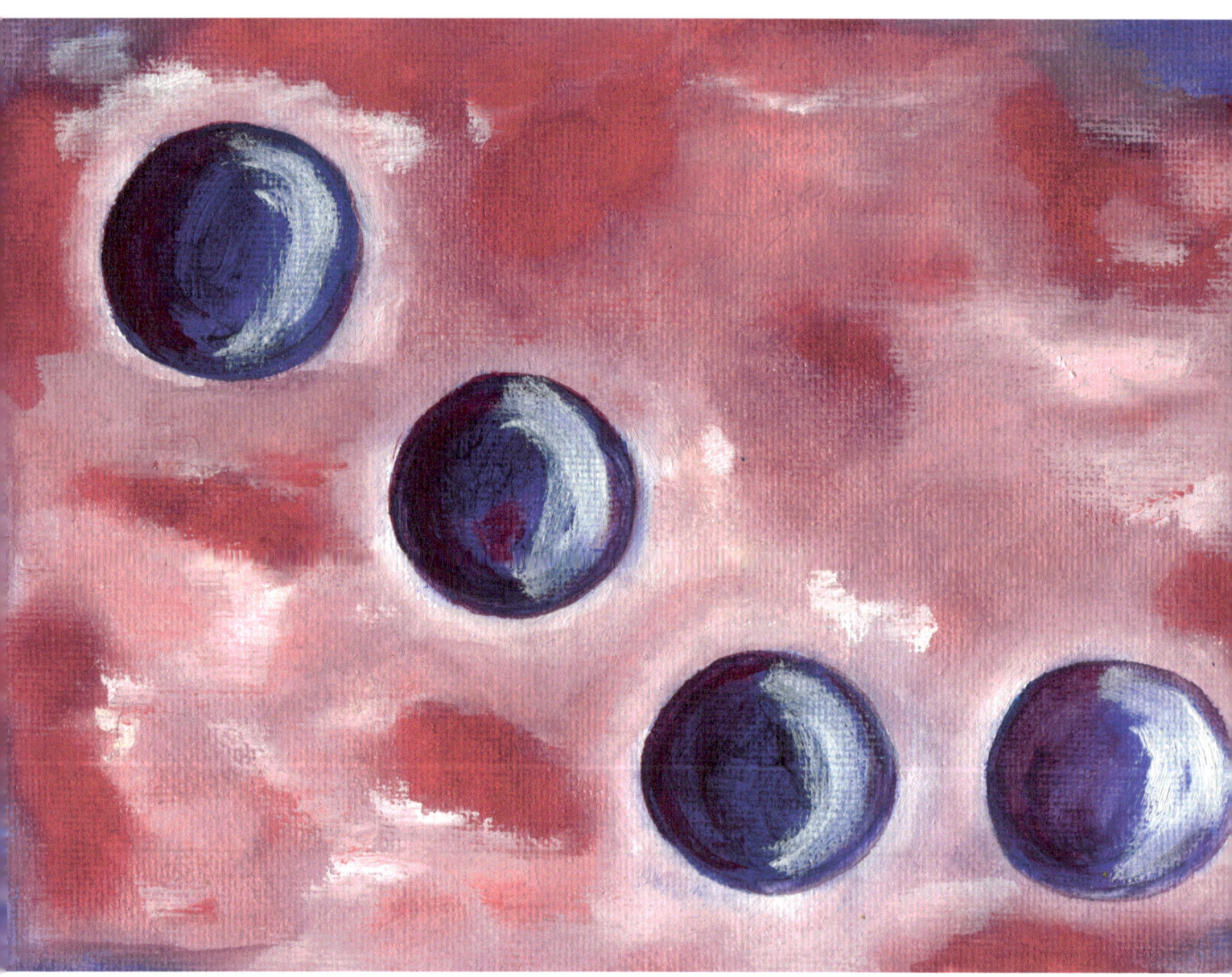

Rise and return...

Pivot a little...

down around and adjourn.

BIG and small Sounds

How to use this book

Each 2-page spread has unique combinations of artwork arranged in pairs of images that represent big and small sounds. They are basic and clear visual representations of loud and quiet sounds. The artwork also makes an excellent starting place for exploring the possibilities of the human voice. Encourage children to imagine the sounds that they hear in the images and how they might make those sounds using their voices. Ask them to consider what vocal sounds they could use, whether the sounds are big or small, and how they might create big or loud sounds and small or quiet sounds. And when you've exhausted the book's possibilities, have the children create their own artwork to represent their understanding, to further explore big and small sounds vocally, instrumentally, and using found sounds. Take it a step further and invite them to experiment with sounds that are not so loud, not so quiet, very loud, and very quiet. The possibilities are endless!

Crow is cawing in the night...

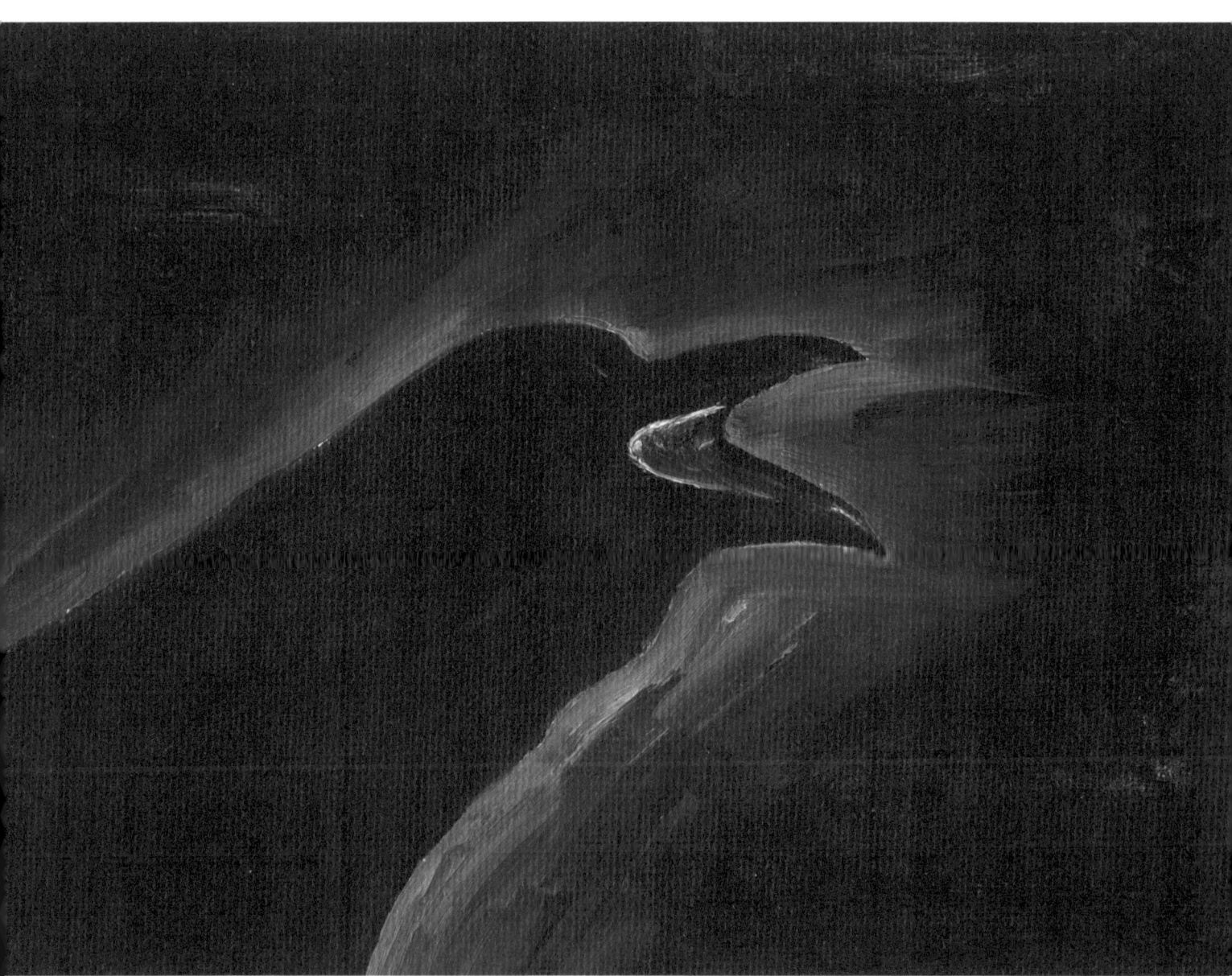

Seagull glides through fading light.

Crashing waves give quite a thrill...

Sunset glows on a sea so still.

Popping corn, a party delight...

Chocolate ice cream, cool and light.

Lips are sealed...

Now in laughter squeal...

Ripe bananas, soft and sweet...

Crunchy carrots, fun to eat.

Balloons float gently in the air...

Popping one gives quite a scare!

Butterfly flutters freely by...

Helicopter chops through the evening sky.

Honking horn can give a fright...

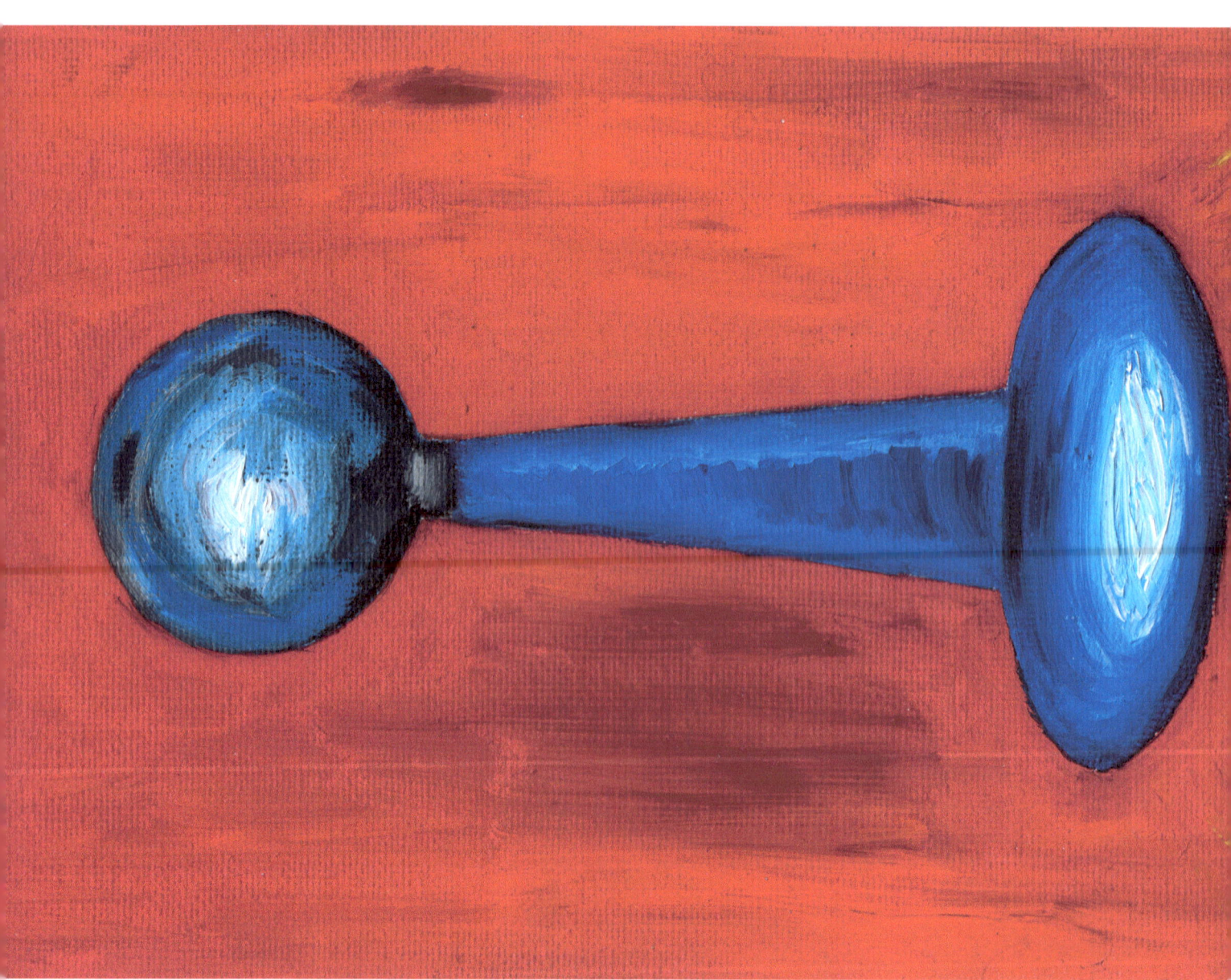

Triangle tings clear and bright.

Surprise! It's a party!

Shhhh! Don't wake the baby.

Lightning cracks through the darkened night...

A starry sky is a wondrous sight.

Fireworks – let's celebrate!

A candle glows upon the cake.

A storm so strong it bends the trees...

Snow sits softly without a breeze.

Sections of Sound

Charlene A. Ryan

How to use this book

Each 2-page spread comprises unique combinations of artwork arranged in patterns that represent typical forms of musical structure. They are basic and clear representations of the overall construction of a composition. The images can be used to introduce and illustrate the concept of musical form. They might be employed to guide focus and understanding while listening to musical works that match the forms represented. The artwork also serves as an excellent starting place for the creation of new musical compositions. Encourage children to imagine the sounds they hear in the images and to differentiate the sounds and musical events in each distinct section of artwork. Ask them to consider what vocal sounds they could use, what found sounds work, and what instrument sounds might be effective. And when you've exhausted the book's possibilities, have the children create their own artwork, as a starting point for their musical creativity to unfold!

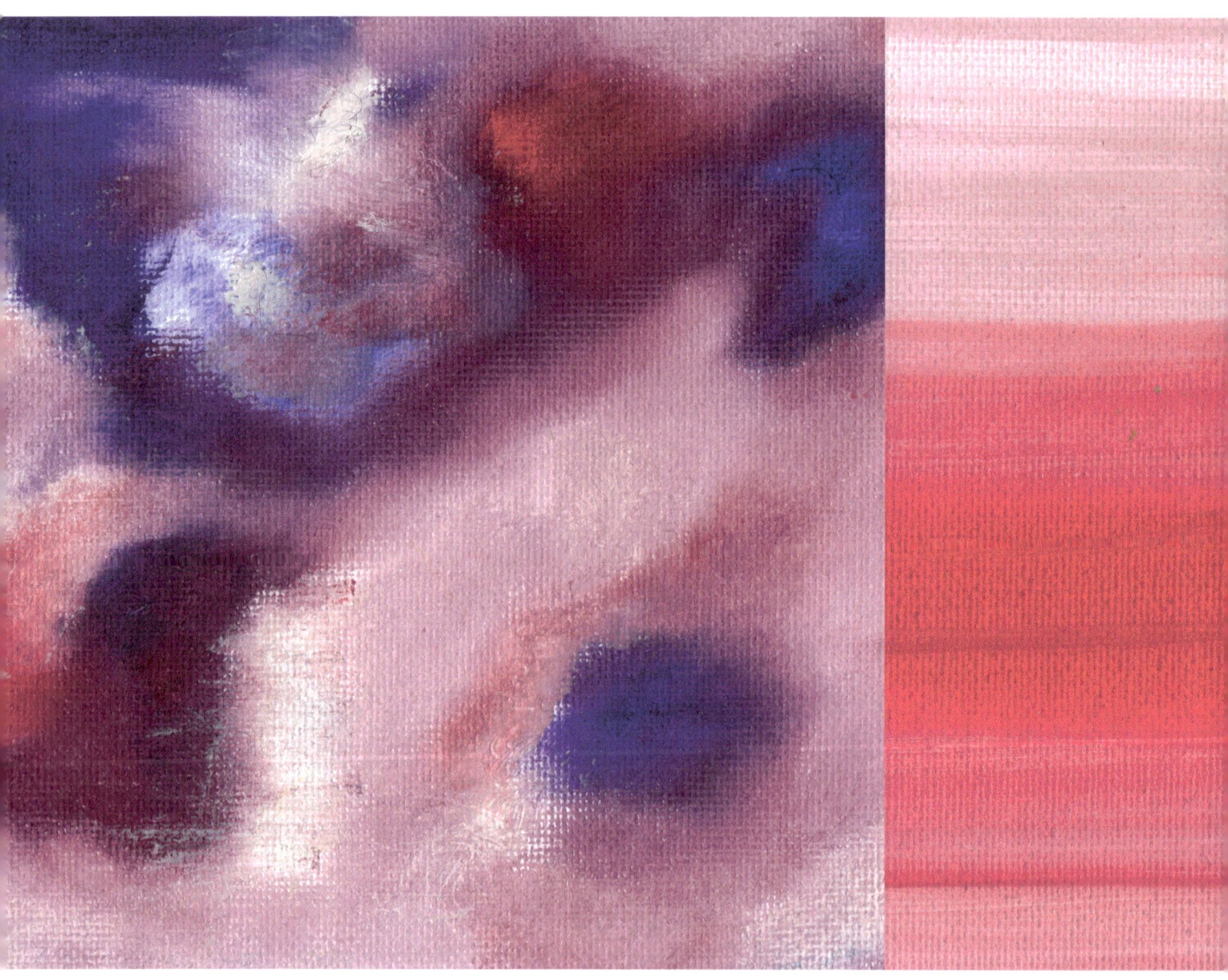

61

FORM: ABA

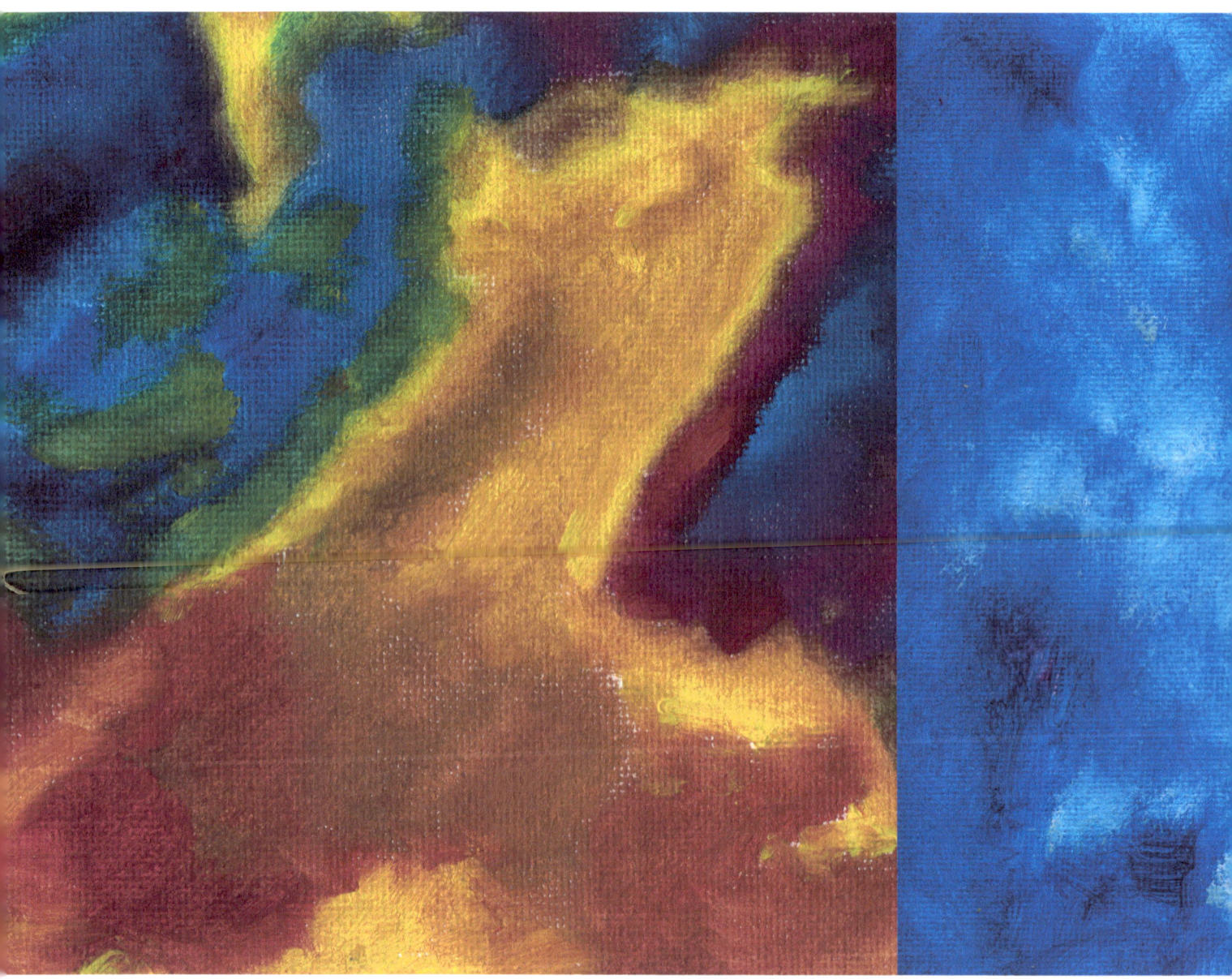

FORM: ABACA

FORM: ABABCB

FORM: AABA

79

Layers of Sound

How to use this book

Each two-page spread is a unique work of art designed to represent the layers of sound that make up a musical composition. The first image at the beginning of the book represents a single musical line. The second image starts as a single line, but another soon joins it. In the third image, there are three lines moving together. As the book progresses, lines enter and leave at different points in the composition and have similar or very different shapes. The artwork provides an aesthetic impetus for engaging students in thinking about the layers that make up a work of music and provide a starting point from which they can explore and create their own. Encourage students to imagine the sounds that could inspire the musical lines and layers, and how they relate to each other. Which lines are more prominent and require more and louder sounds? Which are less prominent and require fewer and quieter sounds? Ask students where higher or lower-pitched sounds might be indicated. And, when you've exhausted the book's possibilities, invite students to create their own artwork as a framework for composing or as a representation of already-composed music, to consolidate their conceptual and practical understanding of musical texture and their aural and visual creativity.

One lovely line...

flowing gently through time.

One to begin and also to end,

but two in the middle, around the bend.

Now there are three...

blending seamlessly.

Three again... but wait...

only one by the end.

Now two... no...

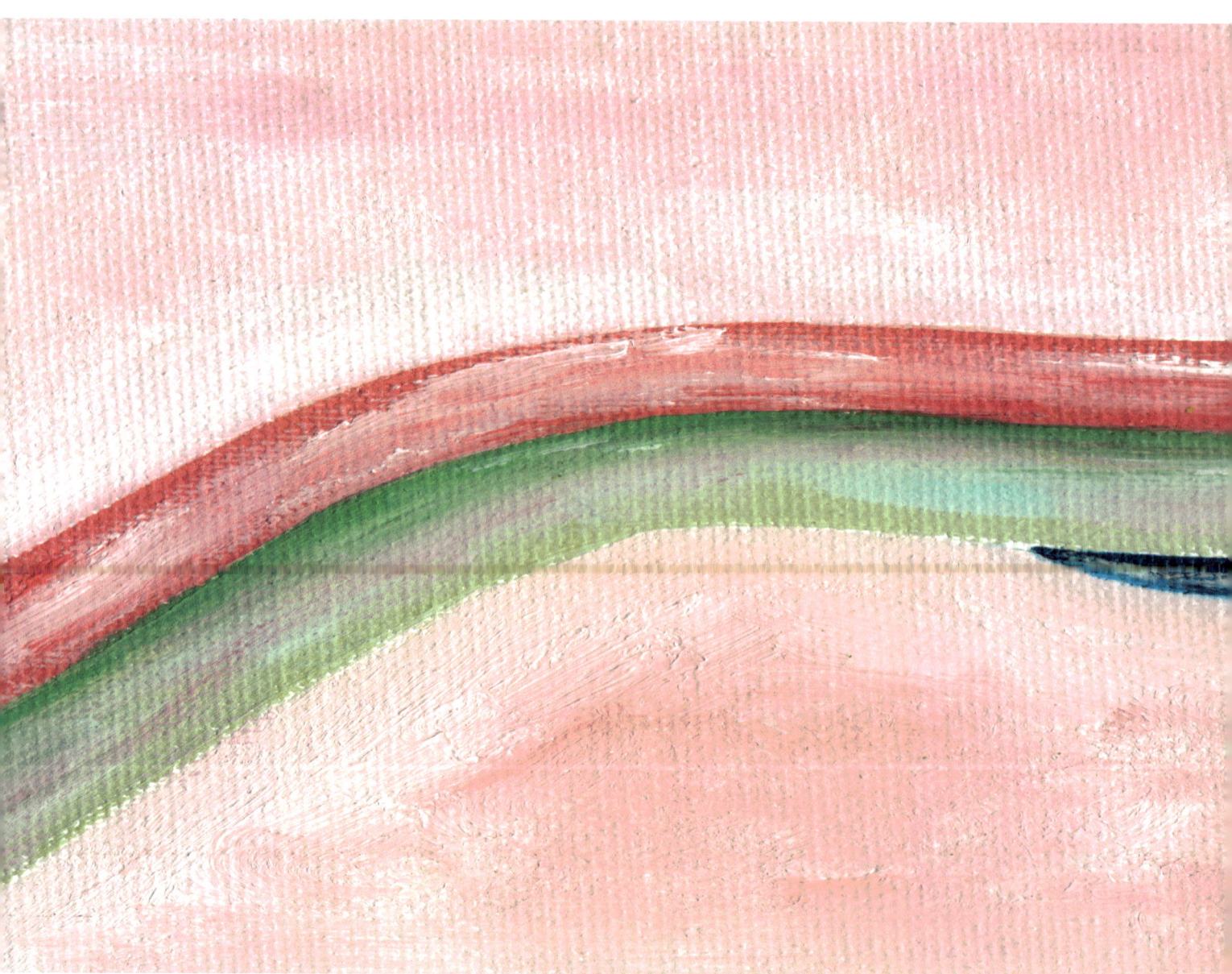

three lines, smoothly flow.

And one, two, three, four...

five sounds grow!

What's this? Three together...

but also apart?

Five at the outset...

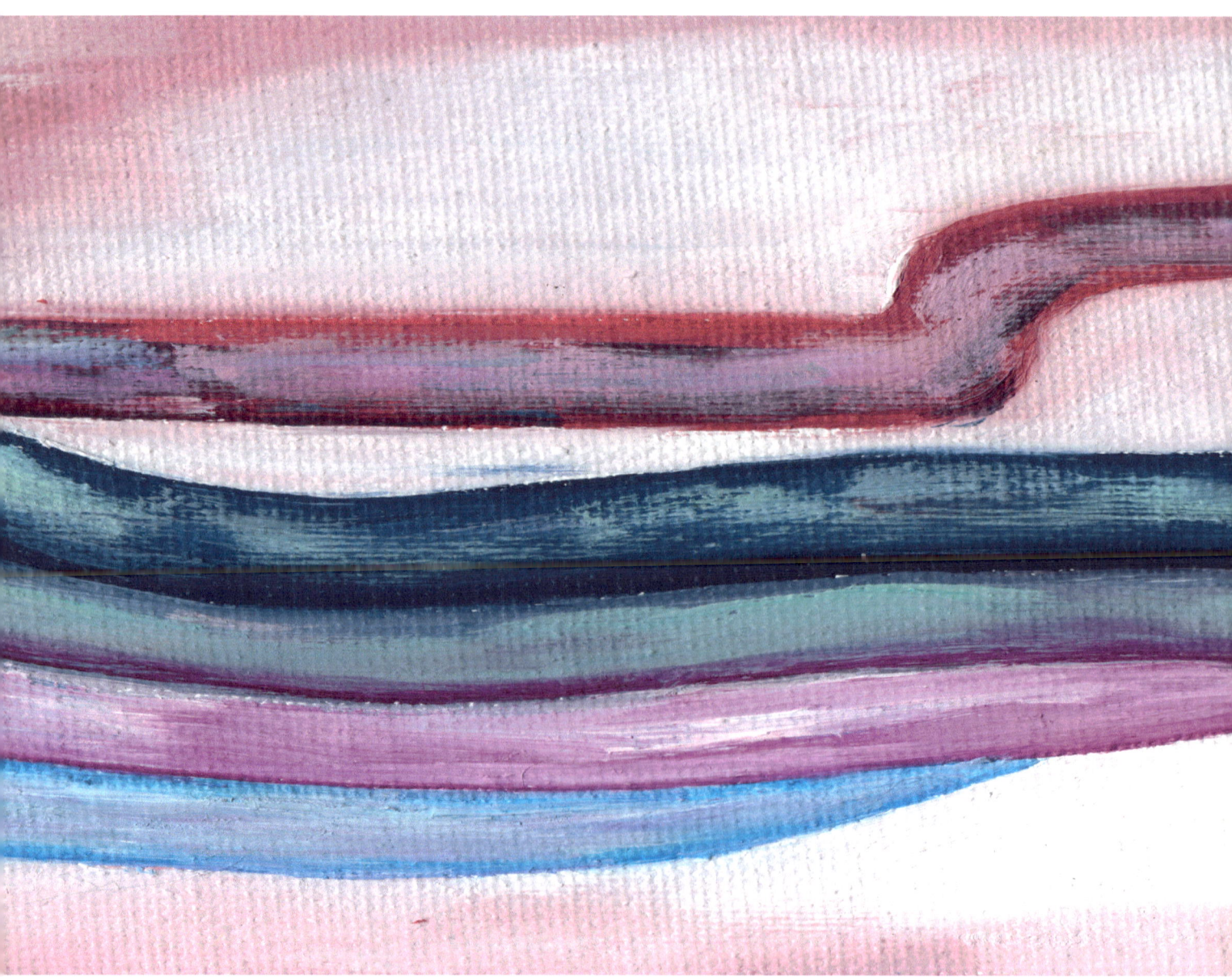

then three depart.

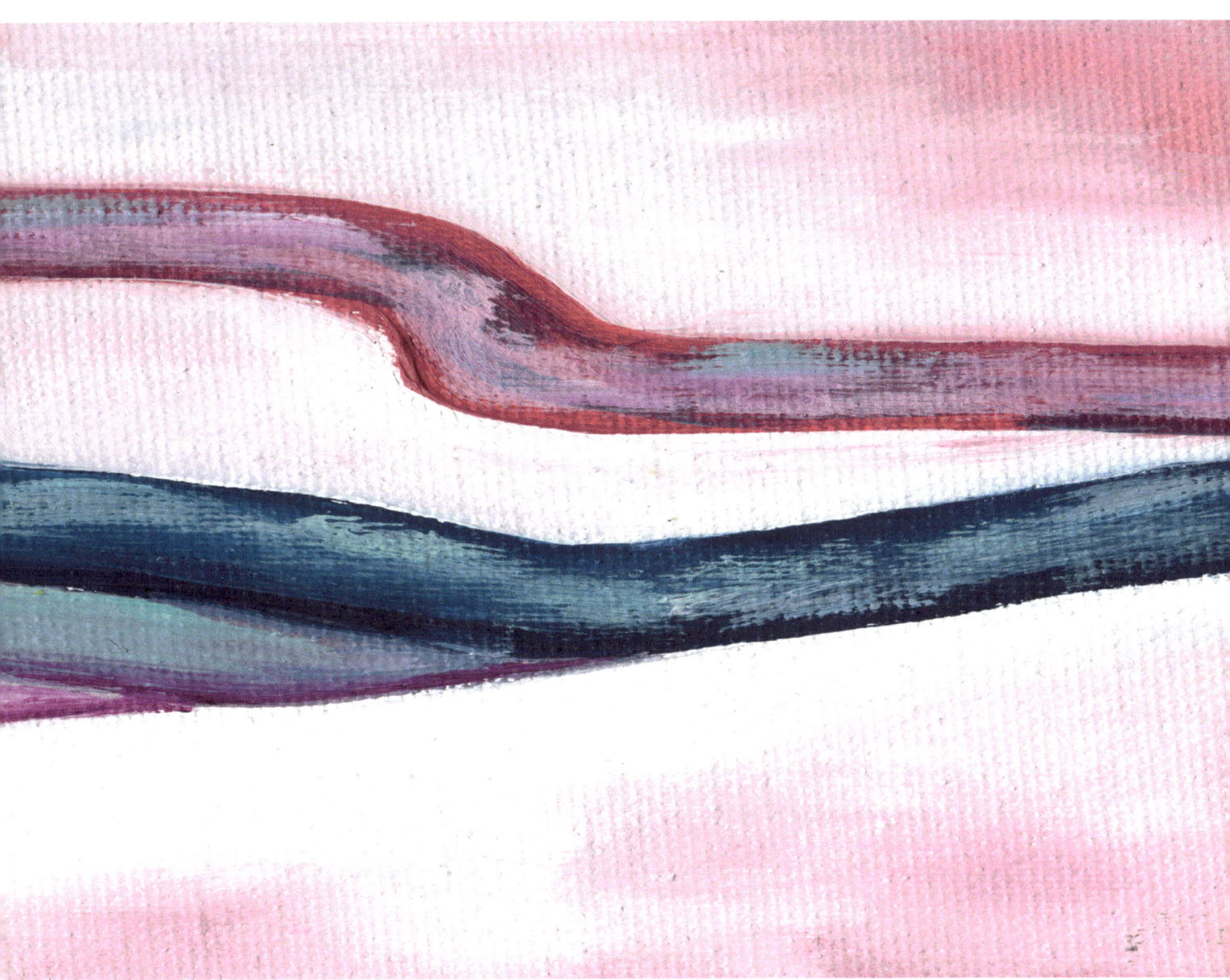

What's happening here?

Five very different...

Only three now...

but surely magnificent.

Is it four? Perhaps...

...more like overlaps.

Now beginning to end...

four lines smoothly blend.

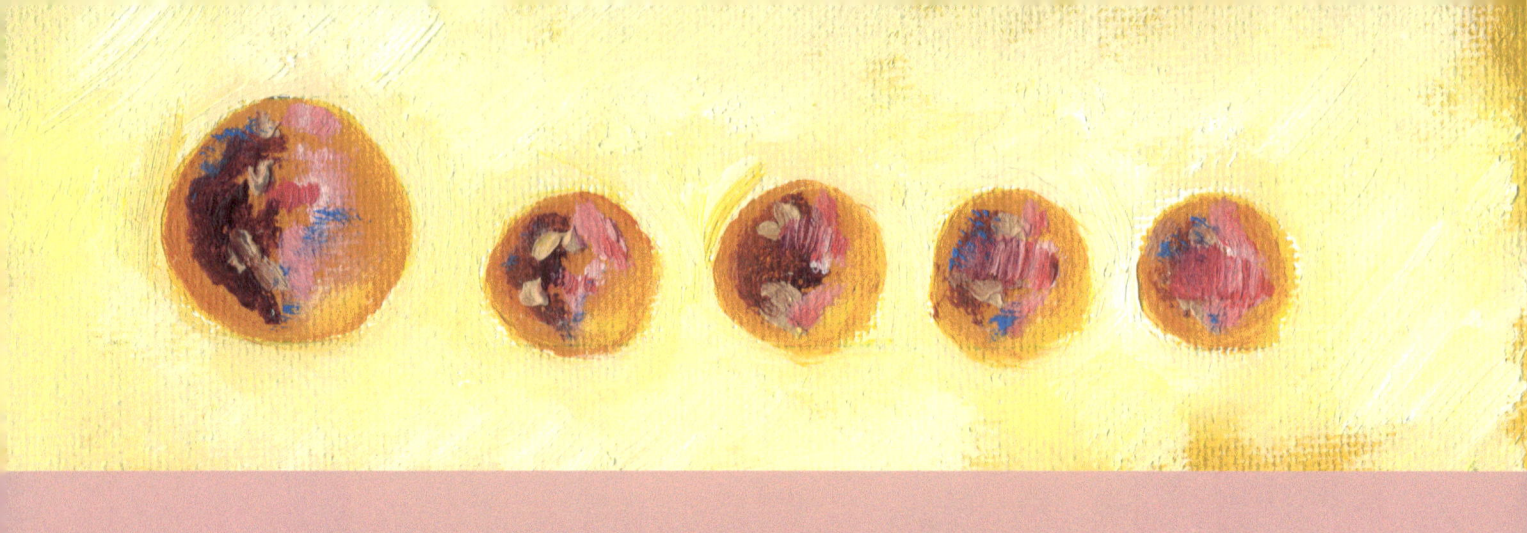

Grouping Sound

Charlene A. Ryan

How to use this book

Each 2-page spread comprises unique works of art designed to represent the grouping of musical sounds — otherwise known as meter. At first, the groupings represent simple unchanging meters — groups of three or four or six, as are often found in musical selections. Later, there are groups of five and seven, less common in some musical circles, but important for building musical flexibility and interest, and for solidifying the concept of musical groupings. Finally, there are groups that represent changing meters, a not uncommon component in musical literature that is often overlooked in discussions and practice of the concept. The artwork provides an aesthetic impetus for engaging children in vocal and instrumental exploration and, importantly, provide clear visual cues as to the emphasis assigned to strong and weak beats. Encourage children to clap, tap, walk, talk or otherwise create the sounds that they hear in the images and to think about how the sounds within one set of images differ from the others. Ask them to create rhythms and melodies that work within each set of images. Then, invite the children to combine their musical and artistic skills by creating artwork to represent meter in the music they create.

PAT pat PAT pat
PAT pat PAT pat...

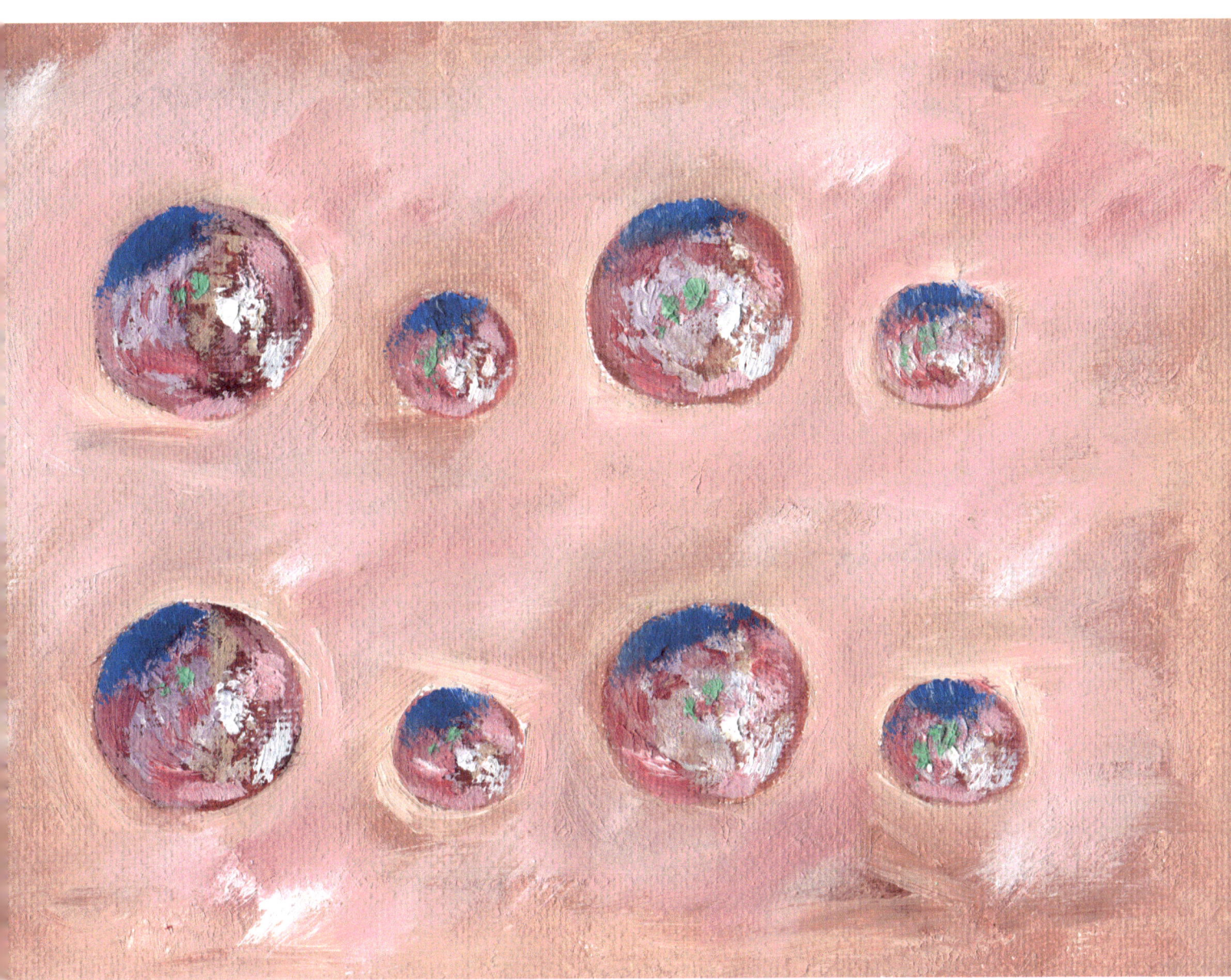

109

CLAP clap clap
CLAP clap clap...

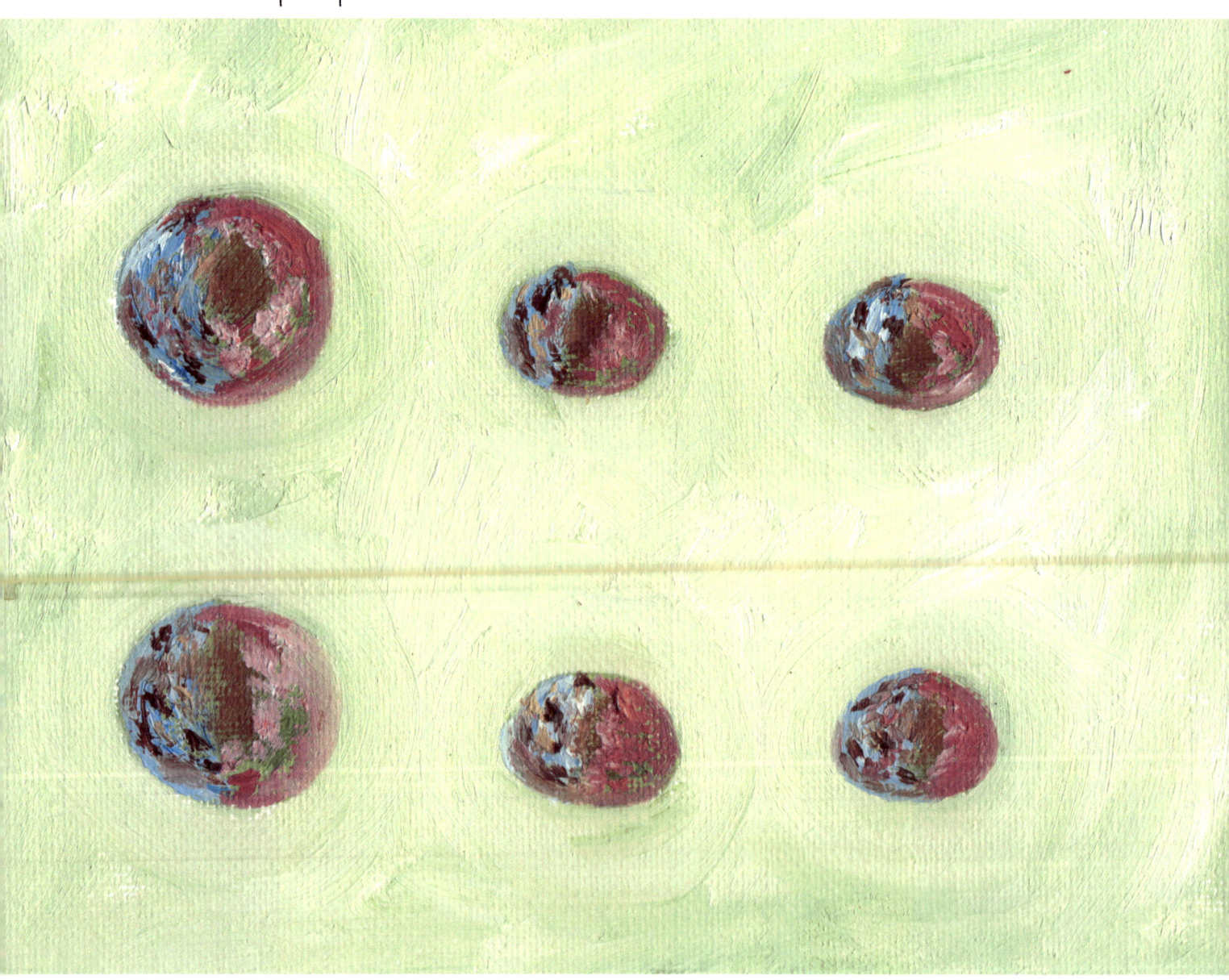

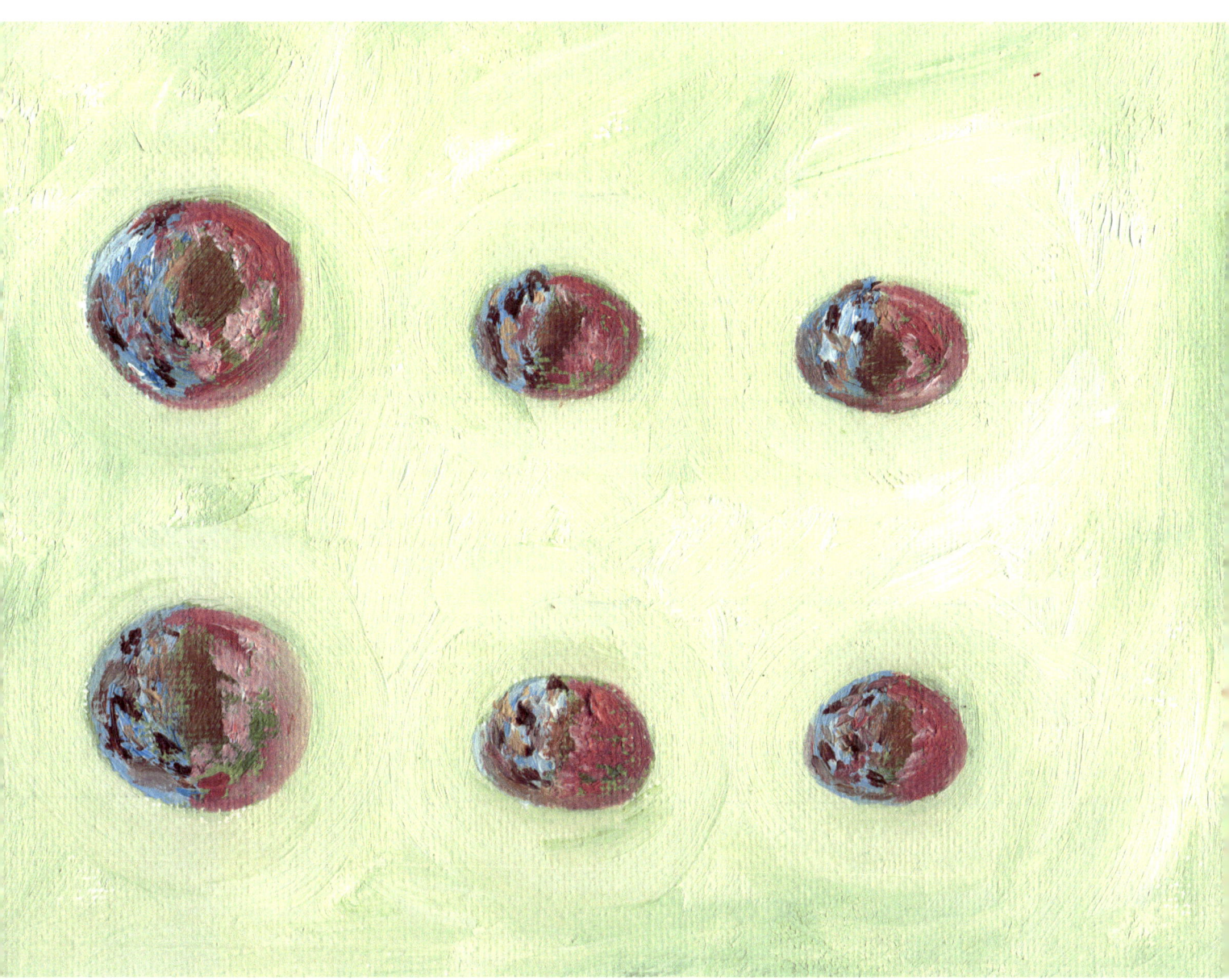

TAP tap tap tap
TAP tap tap tap...

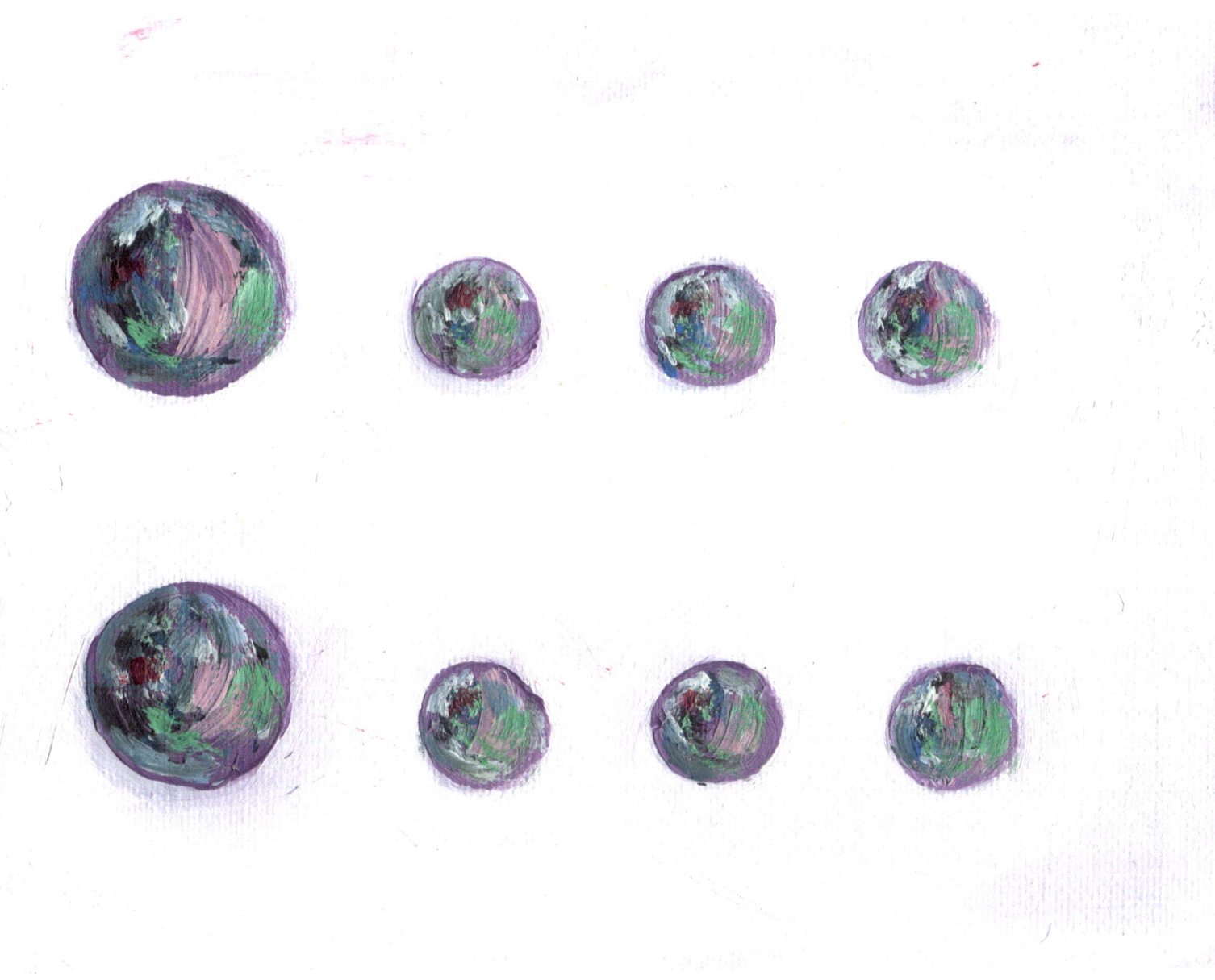

STEP step step step step
STEP step step step step...

PAT pat pat PAT pat pat
PAT pat pat PAT pat pat...

CLAP clap clap clap clap clap clap
CLAP clap clap clap clap clap clap...

119

TAP tap
TAP tap tap...

STEP step step
STEP step step step...

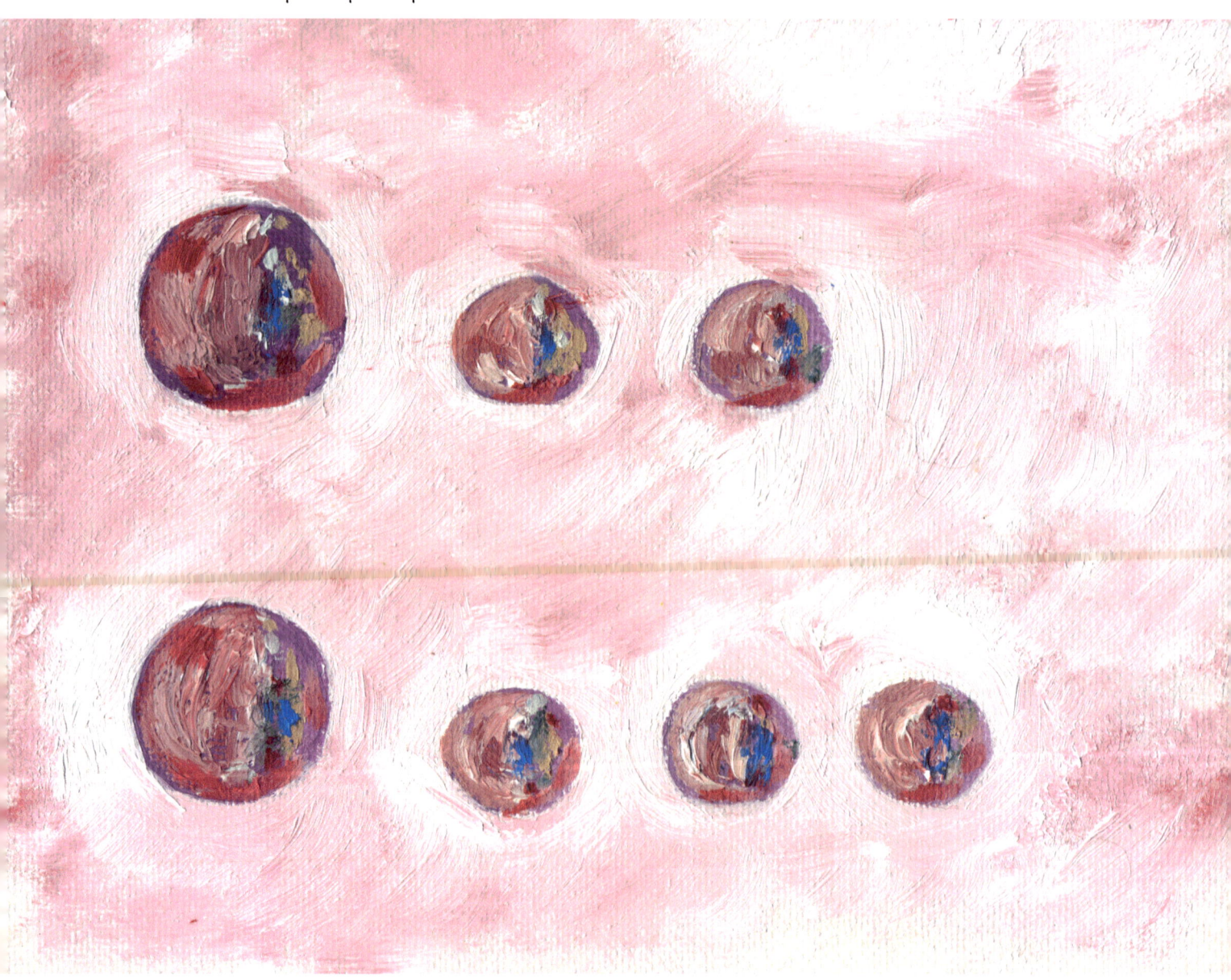

PAT pat pat pat
PAT pat pat pat pat...

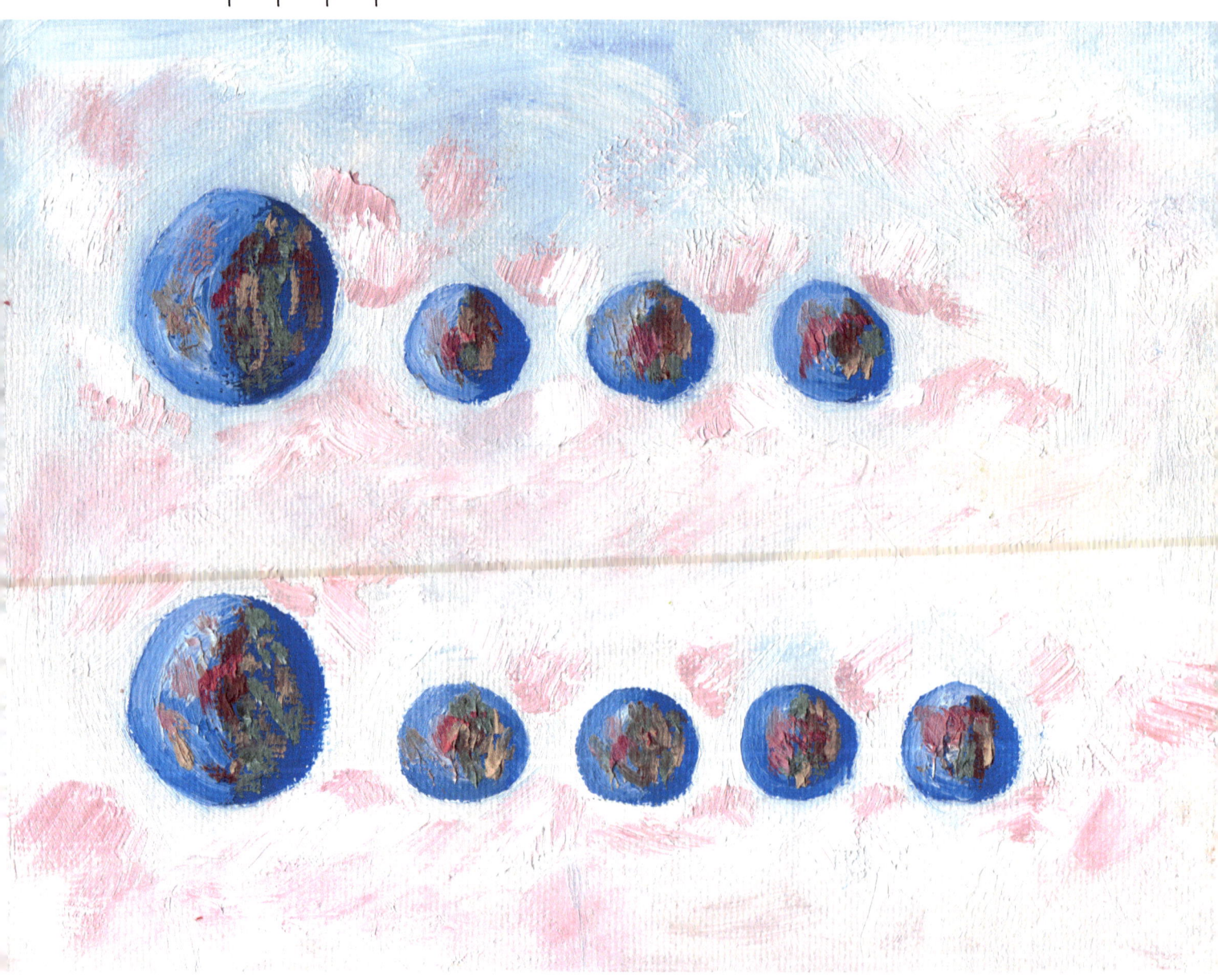

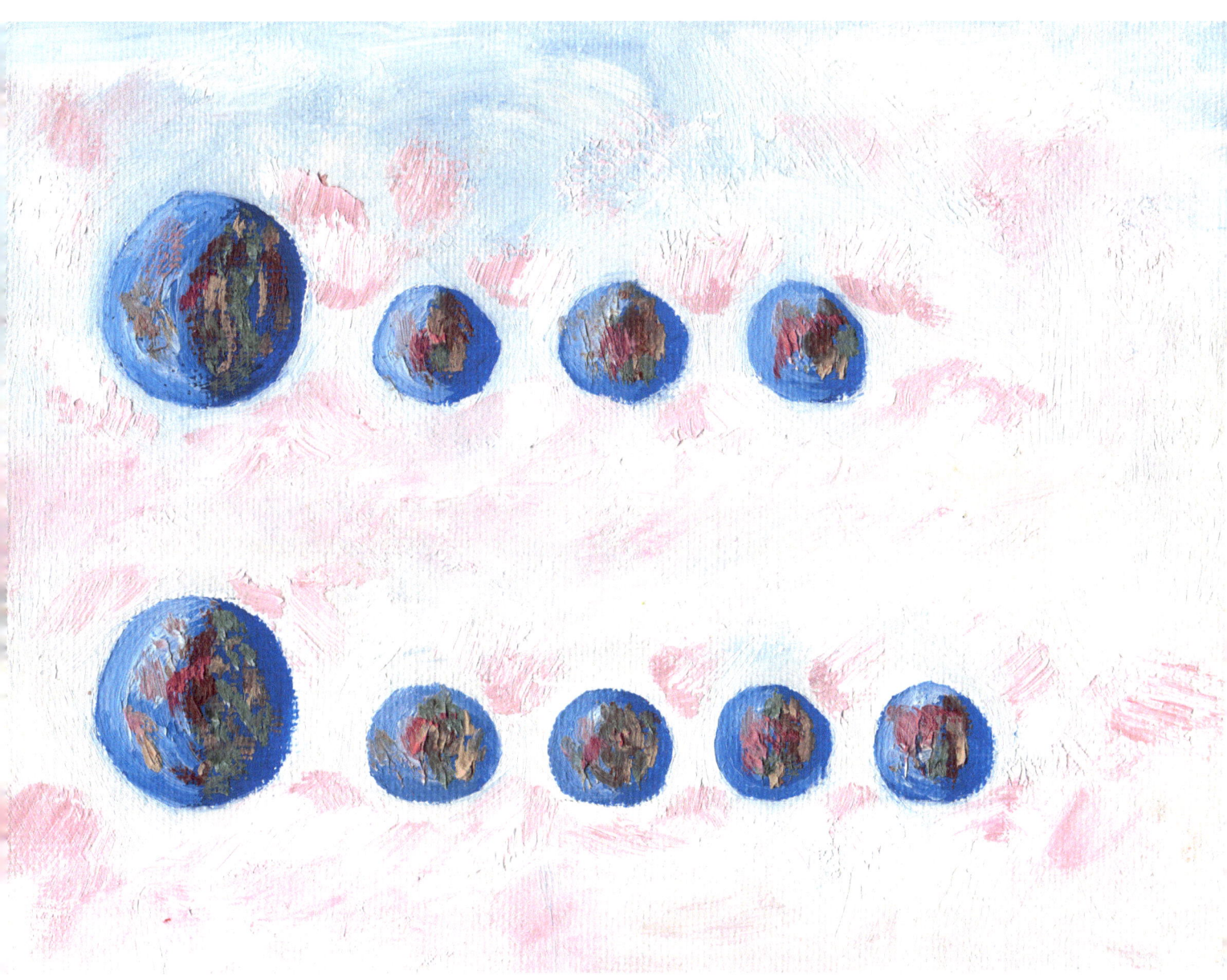

CLAP clap CLAP clap
CLAP clap clap clap clap...

TAP tap TAP tap
TAP tap tap tap...

STEP step step
STEP step step step step...

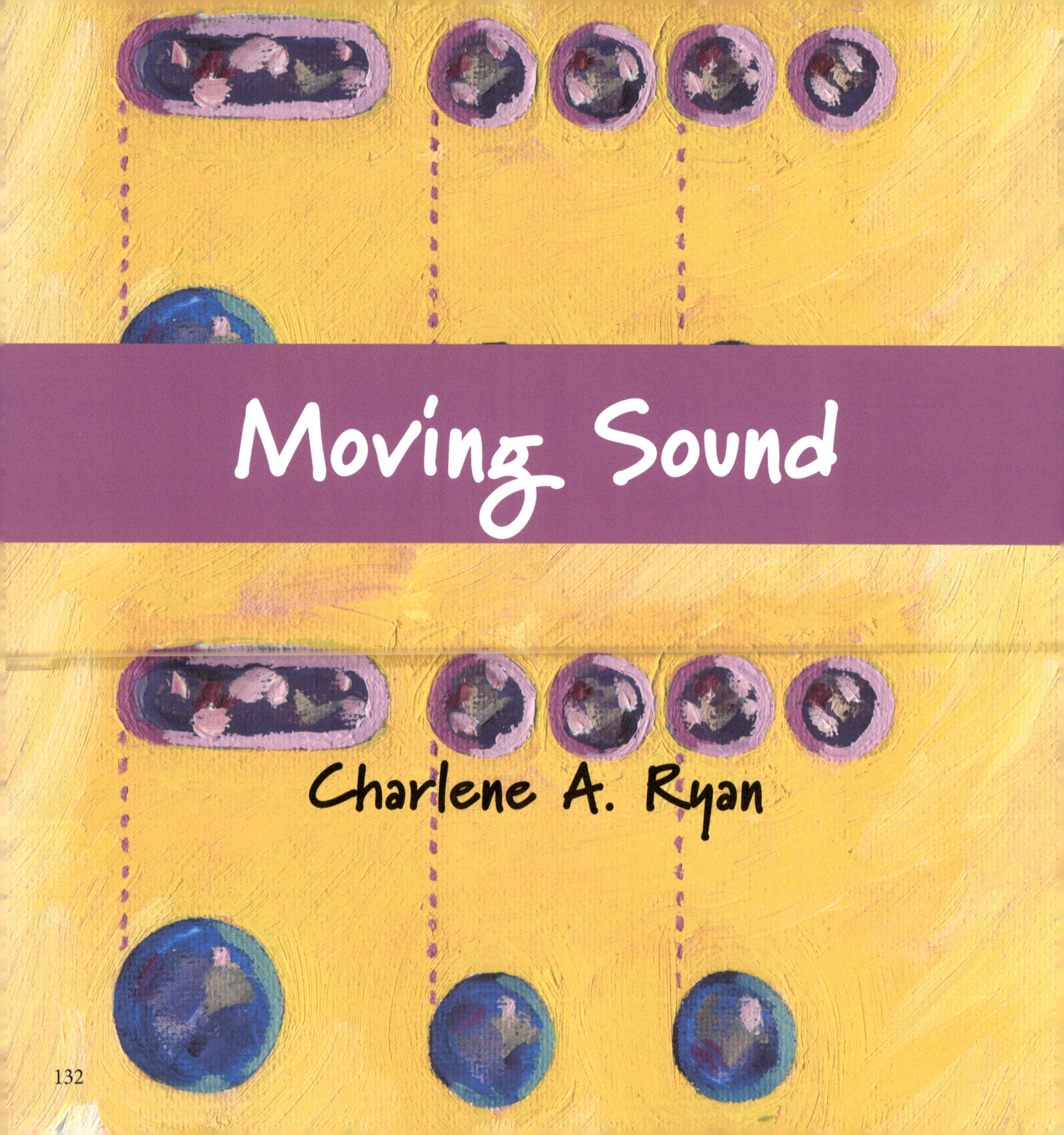

Moving Sound

Charlene A. Ryan

How to use this book

Each page is a unique work of art designed to represent the ways that sounds are arranged to move through time – combining rhythm for interest, beat as the driving force, and meter as the framework. The images on each page combine these three elements using simple representations of bigger/smaller, and longer/shorter shapes. The two lines work together simultaneously: the top representing rhythm and the bottom representing beat; meter is woven across both lines. Invite learners to explore the steady pulse of the beat with their voices and bodies, making the bigger shapes louder than the smaller. Have them investigate the different lengths of sounds in the rhythms. Invite them to work with you or in groups – one performing the beat and the other performing the rhythm. Encourage learners to discover how the bigger shapes define groups of beats (meter) within which the rhythms move, and note how these three musical elements (beat, rhythm, meter) work together to move us and the music along!

Loo-ooh lol-ly lol-ly

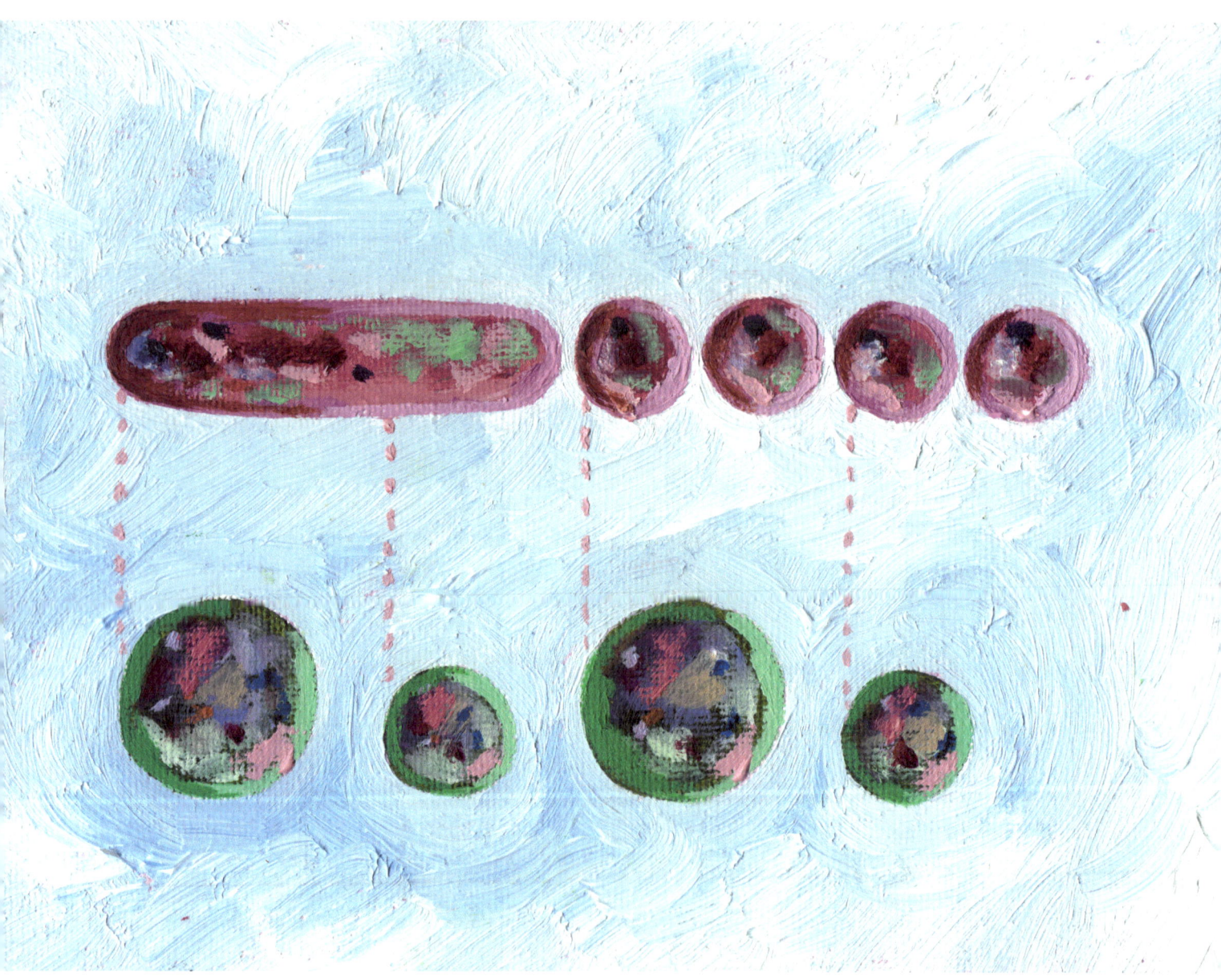

STEP step STEP step

Lol-ly loo lol-ly loo

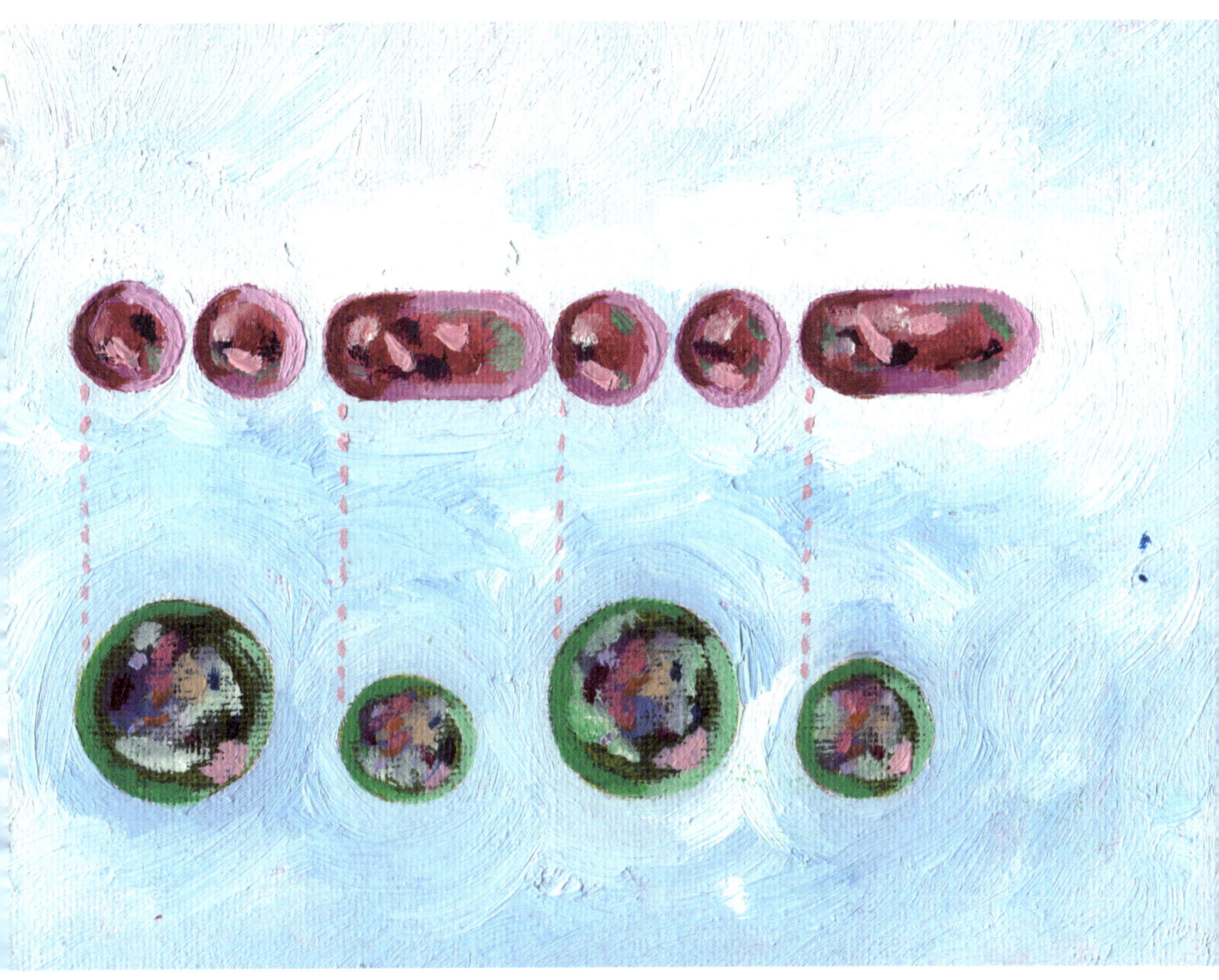

STEP step STEP step

Loo lol-ly loo lol-ly

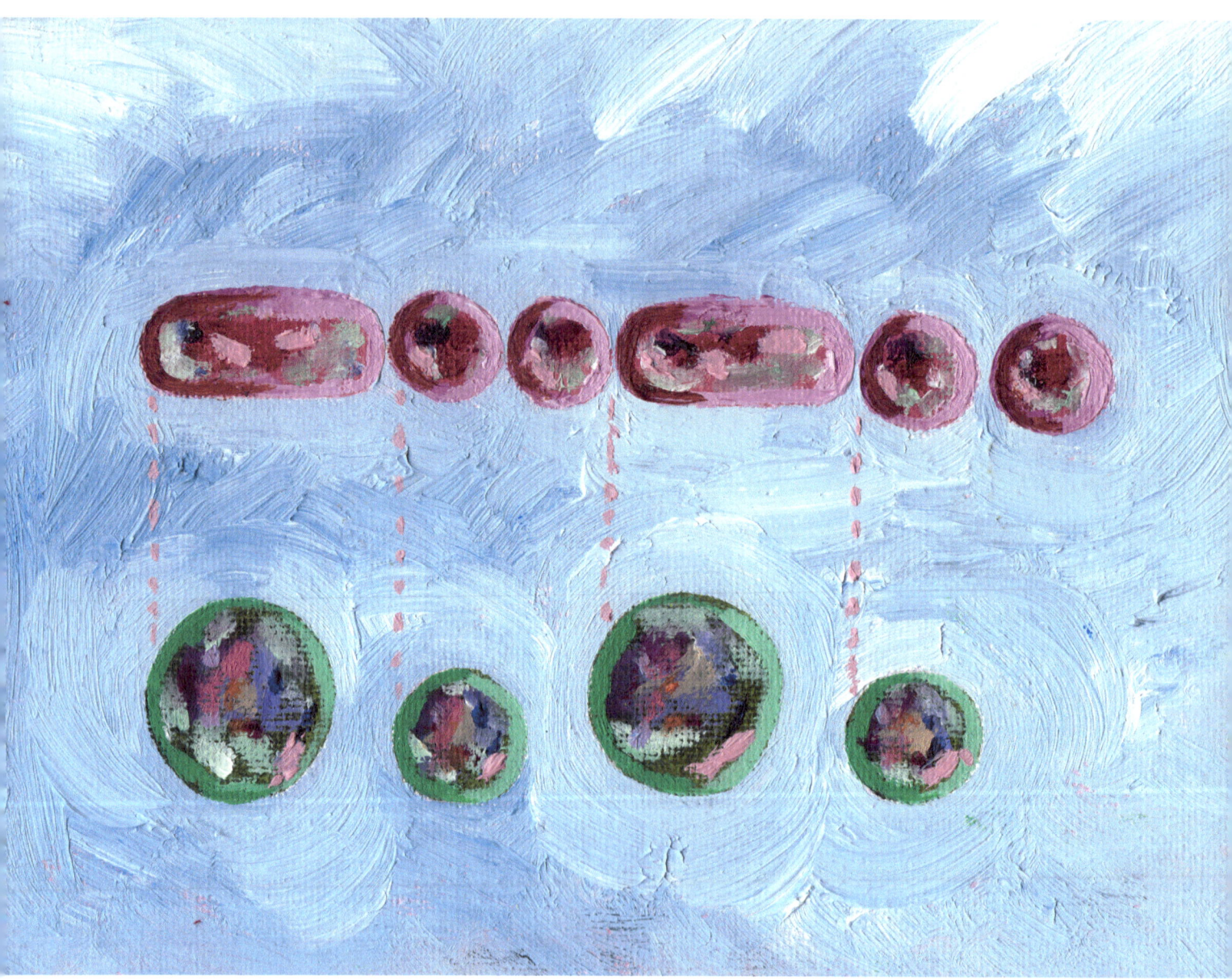

STEP step STEP step

Lol-ly loo lol-ly loo

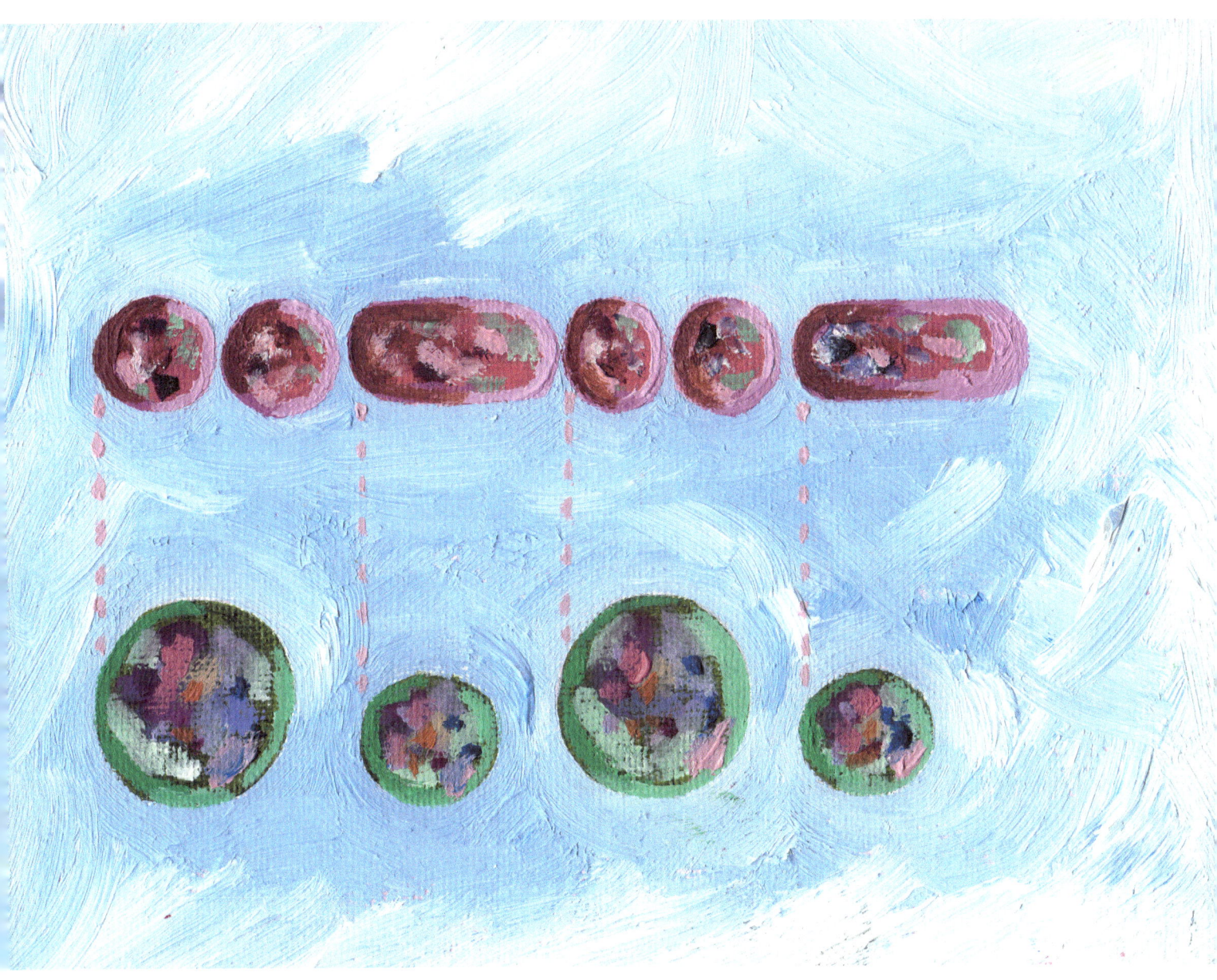

STEP step STEP step

137

Lol-ly loo lol-ly loo

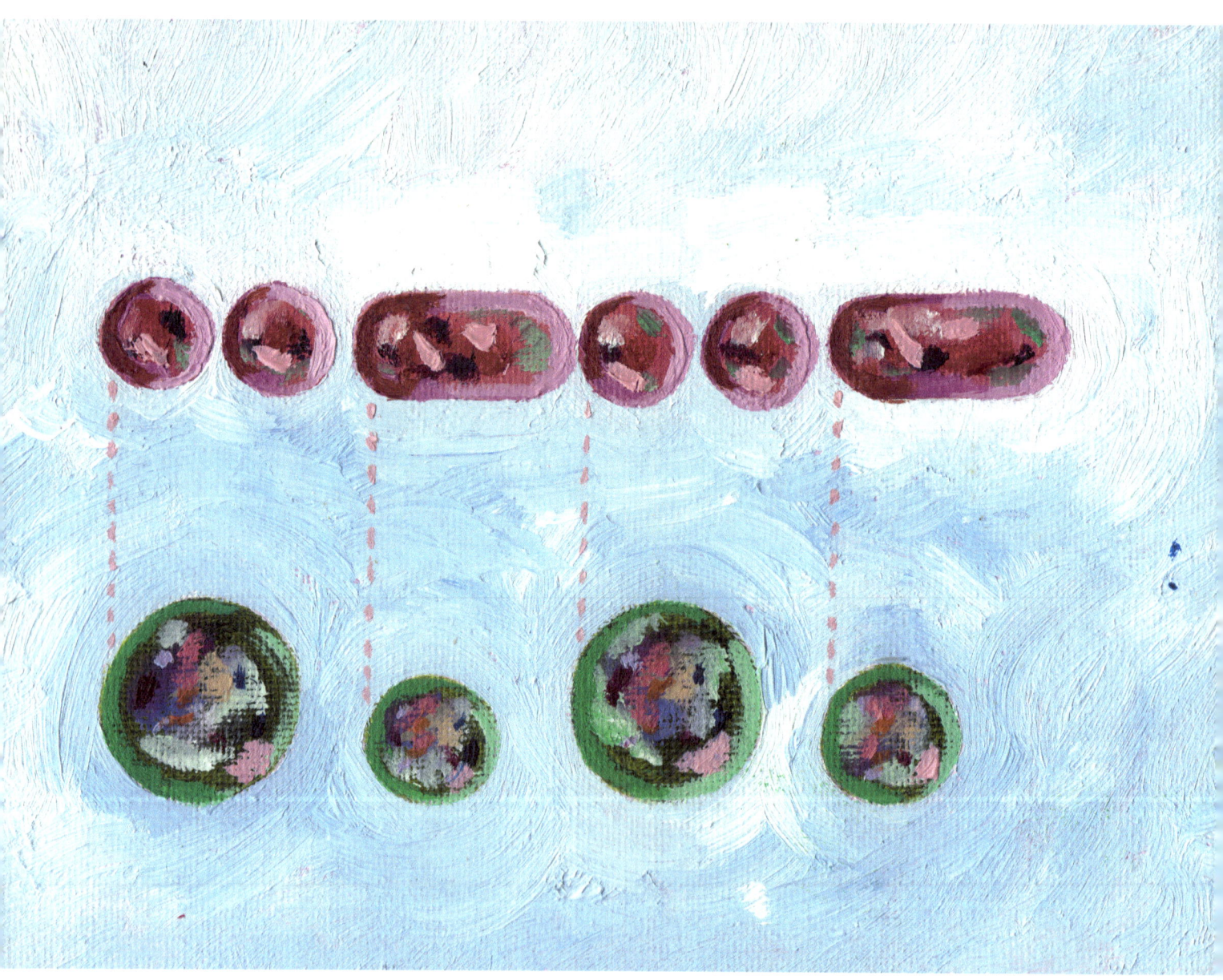

STEP step STEP step

138

Loo lol-ly loo lol-ly

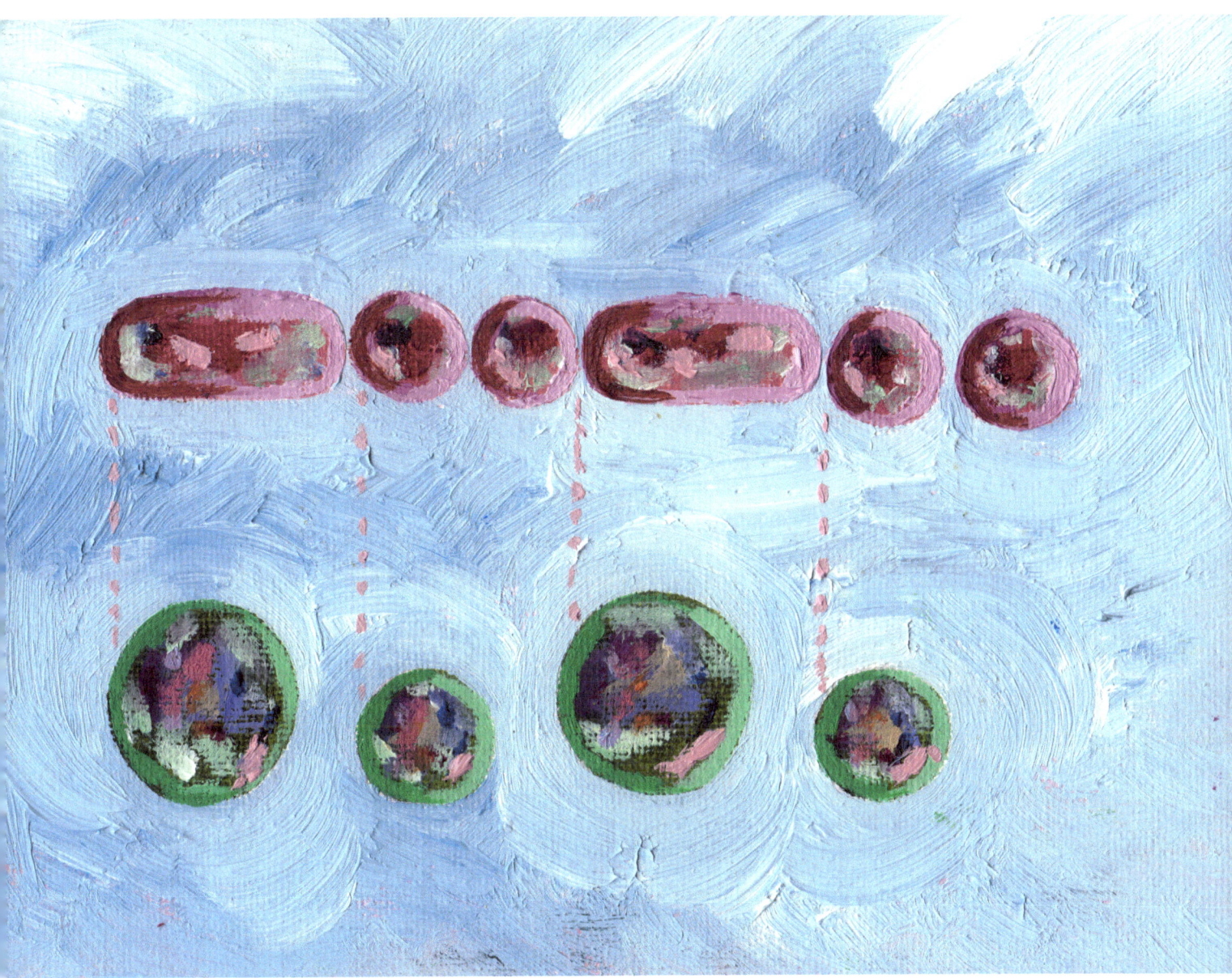

STEP step STEP step

Lol-ly loo lol-ly loo

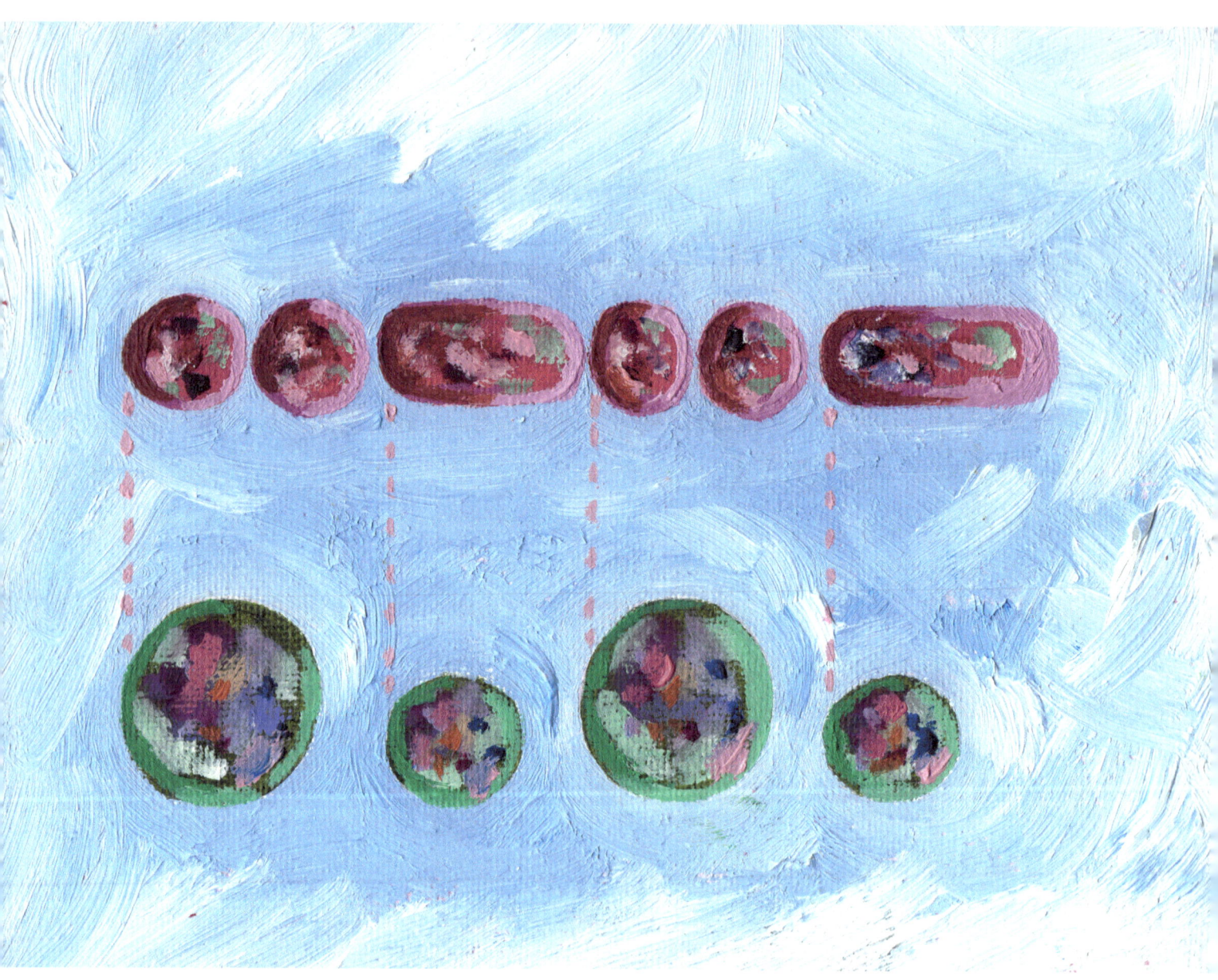

STEP step STEP step

Loo-ooh   lol-ly   lol-ly

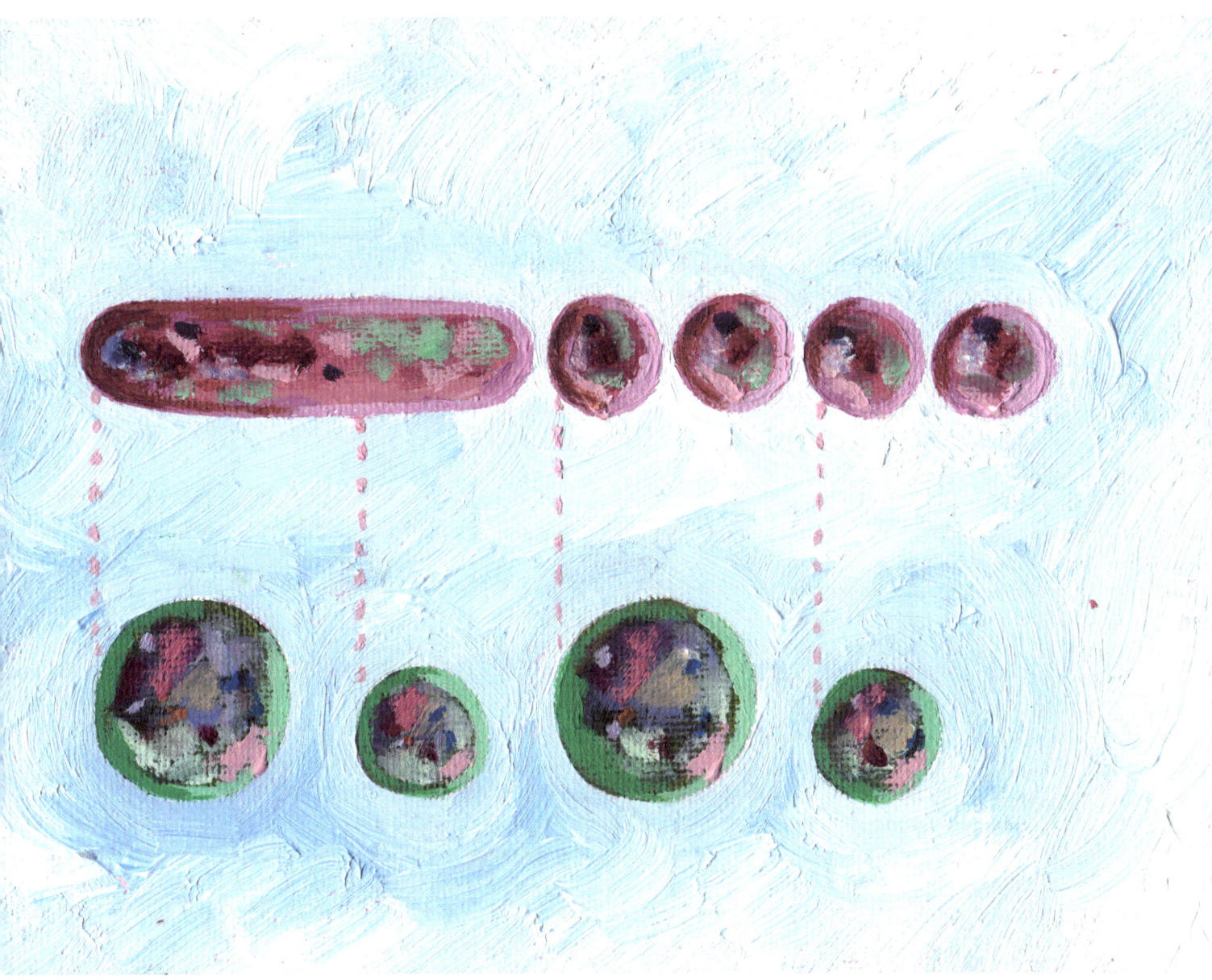

STEP step STEP step

Tip-py tip-py tip-py

CLAP clap clap

Tip-py tip-py tap

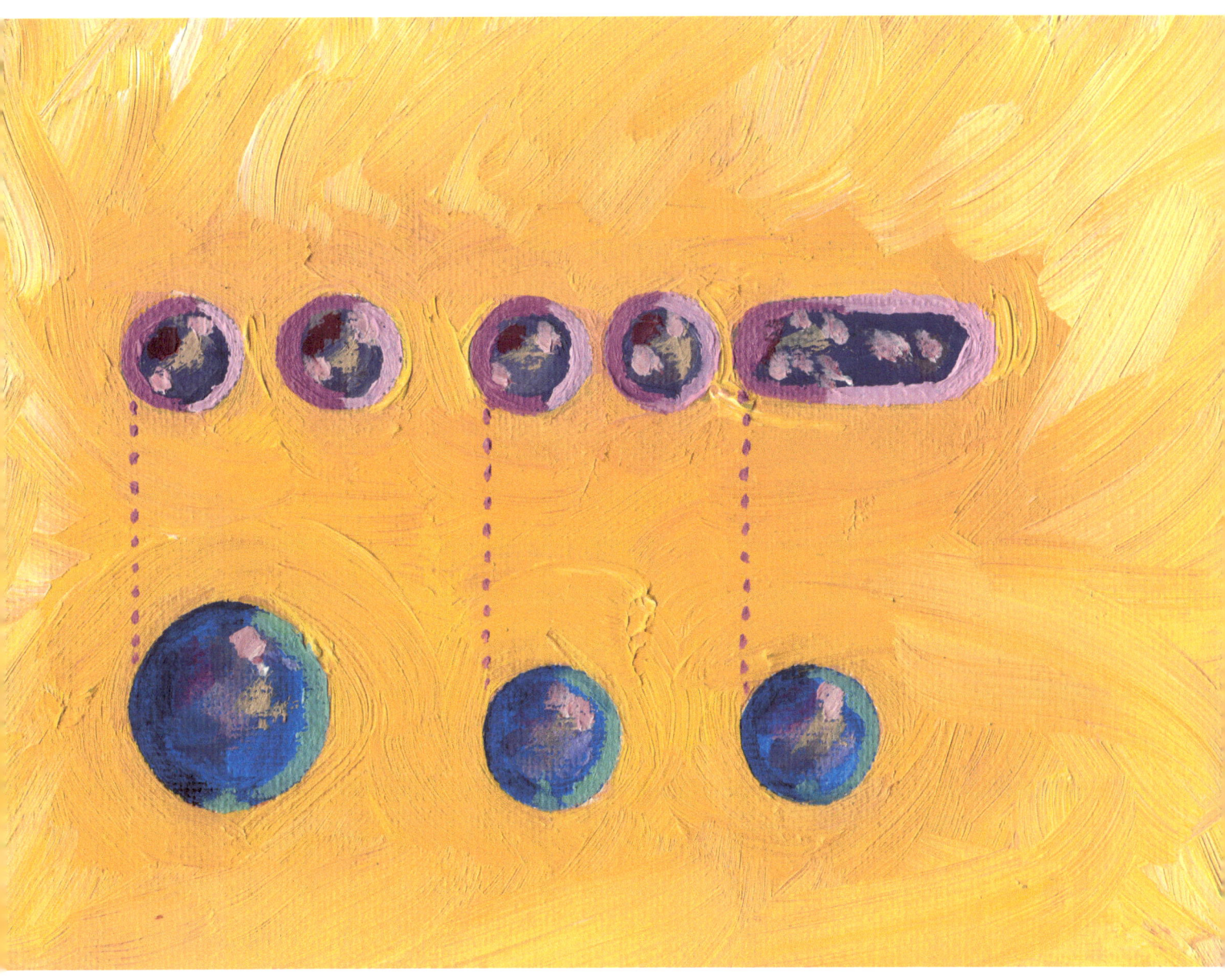

CLAP clap clap

Tip-py tap tip-py

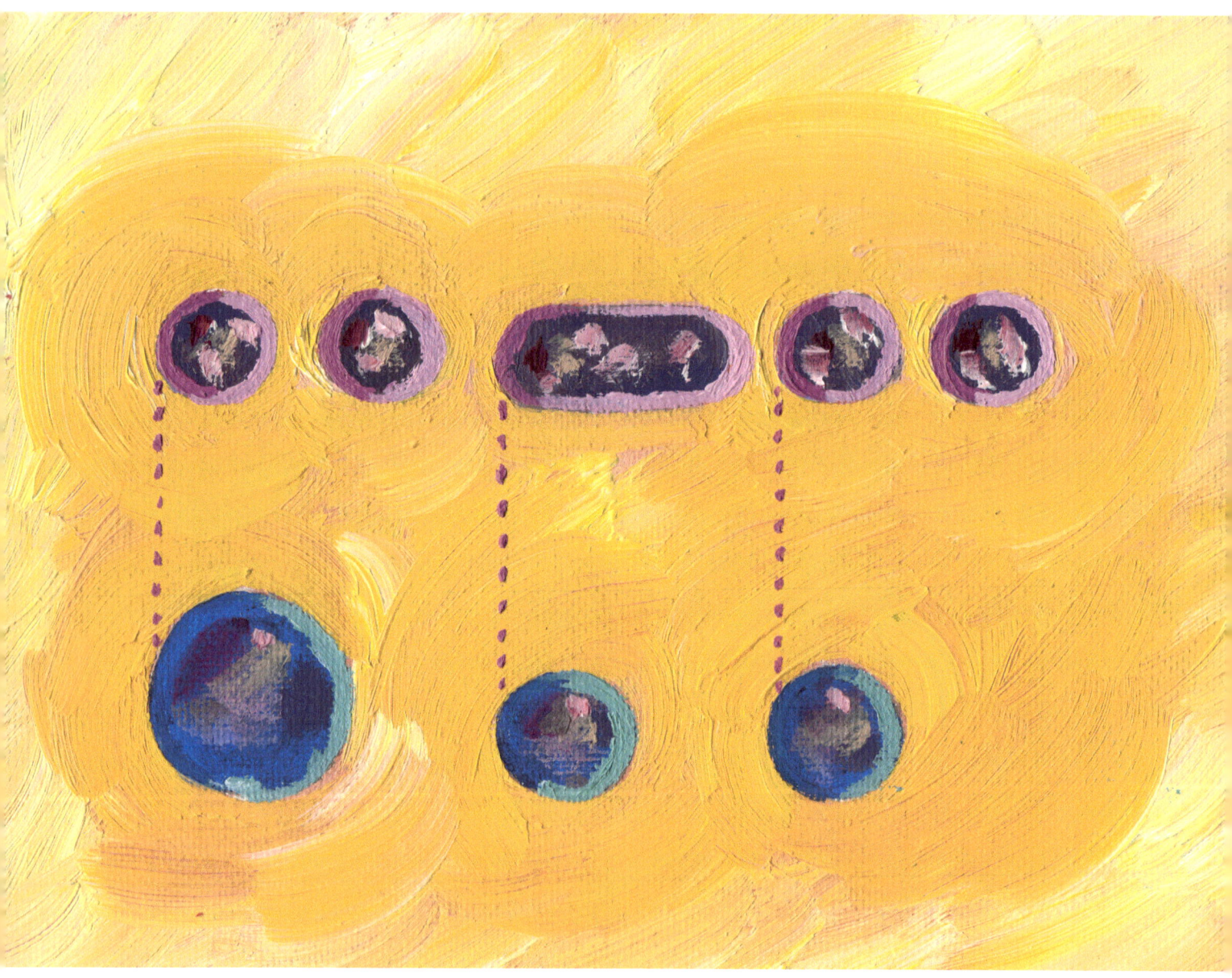

CLAP clap clap

Tap tip-py tip-py

CLAP clap clap

Tip-py tip-py tap

CLAP clap clap

Tip-py   tap   tip-py

CLAP clap clap

Tap tip-py tip-py

CLAP clap clap

Tip-py tip-py tip-py

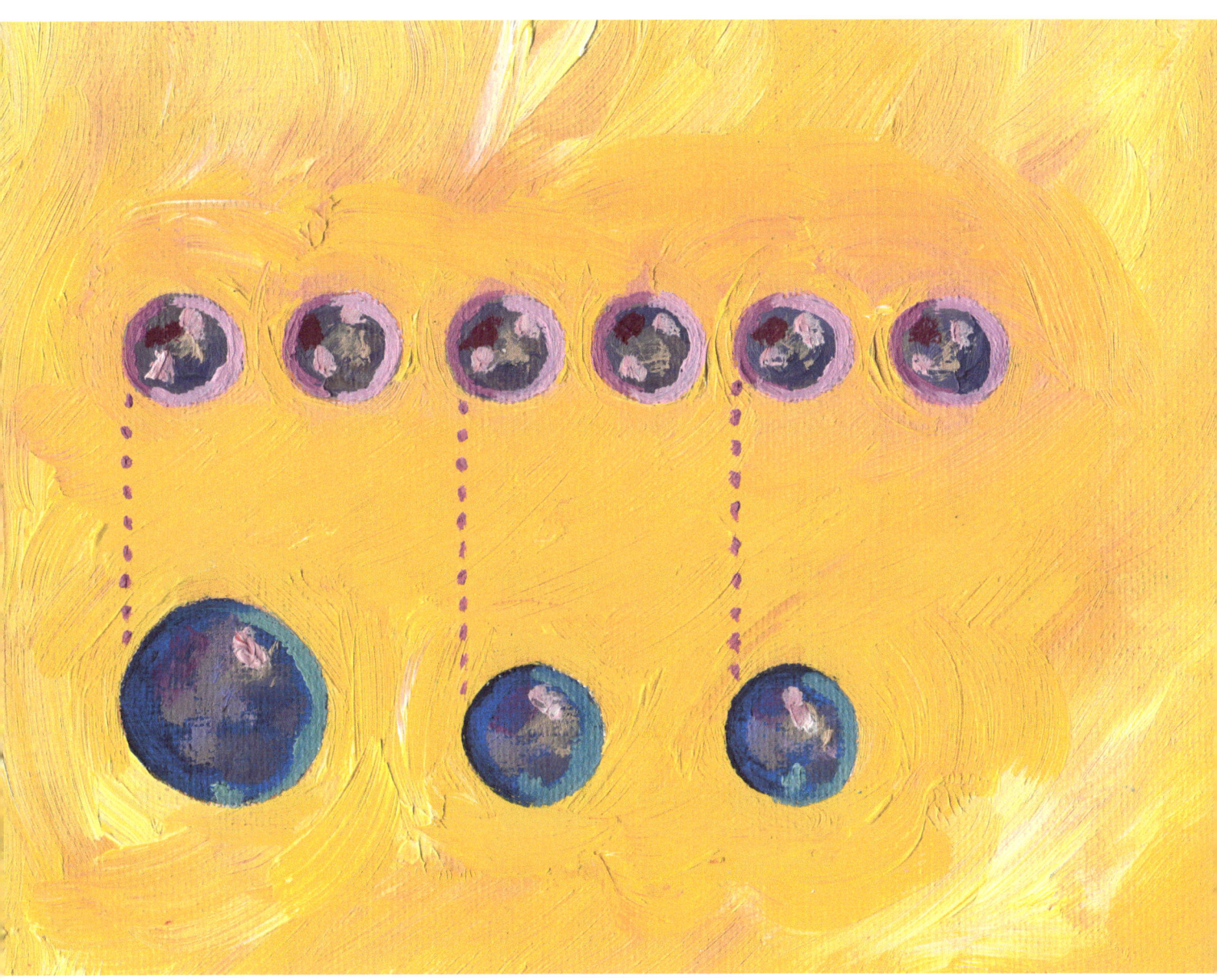

CLAP clap clap

Pop-py pop-py pay pop-py

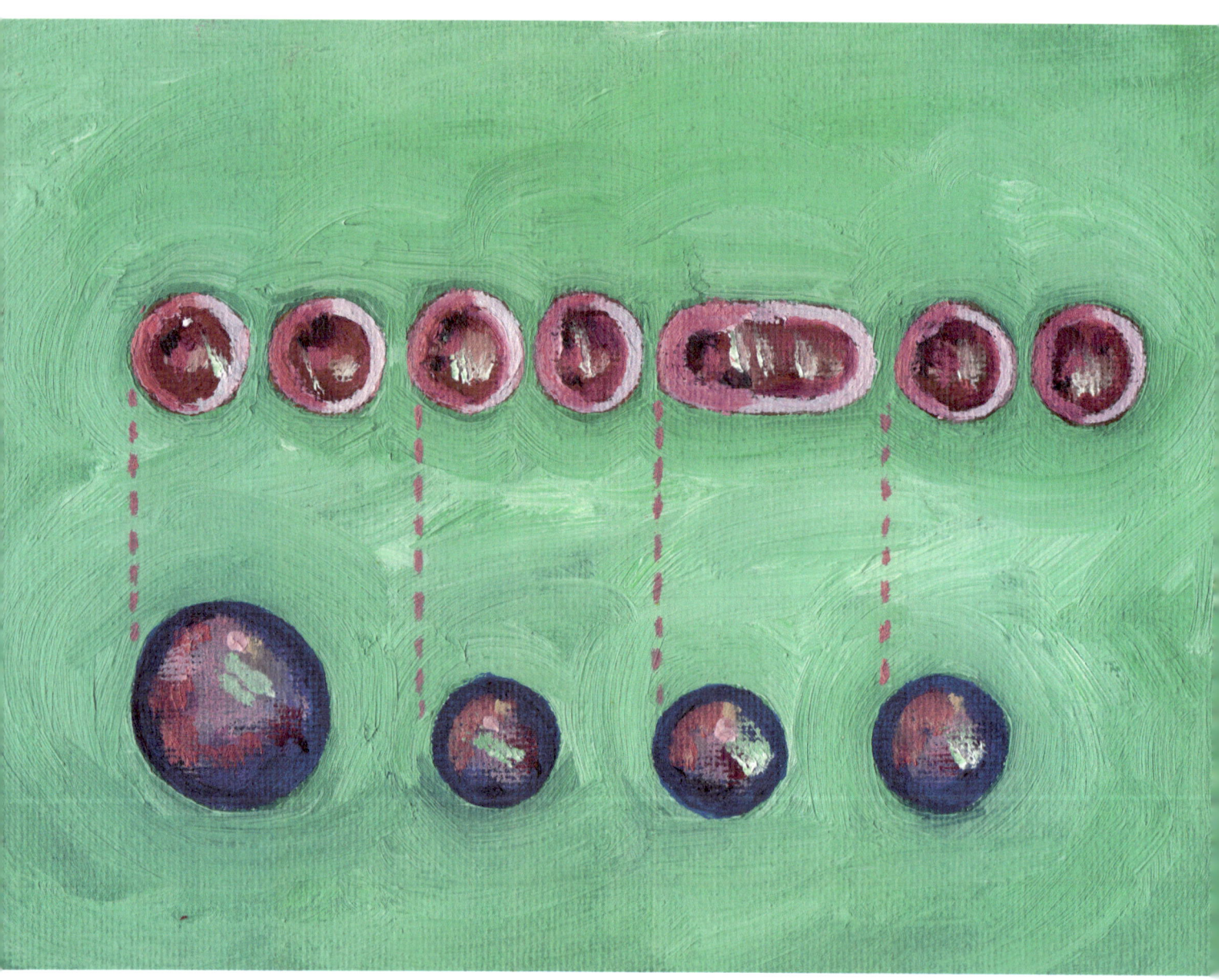

SNAP snap snap snap

Pop-py pop-py pop-py pay

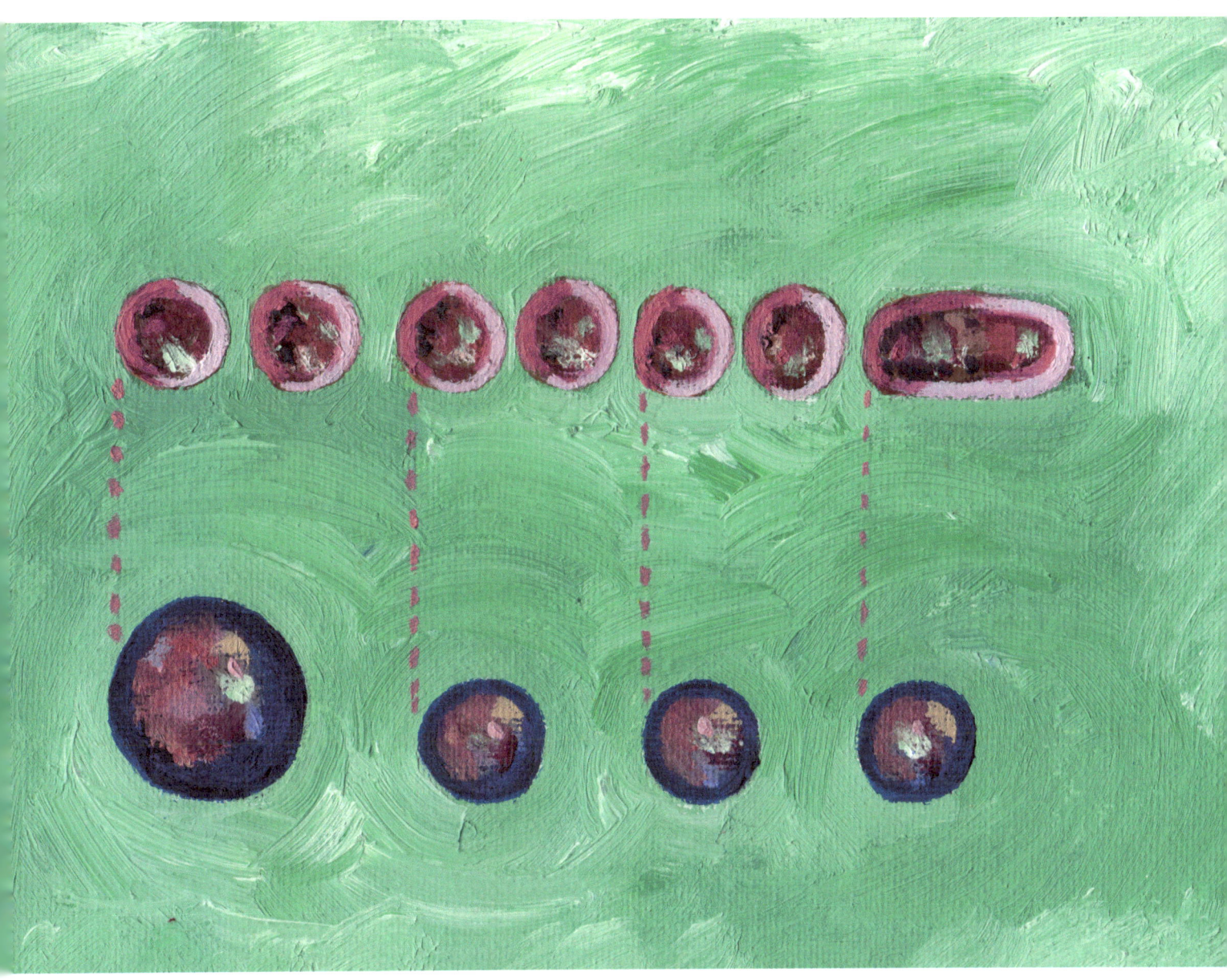

SNAP snap snap snap

Pay pop-py pop-py pay

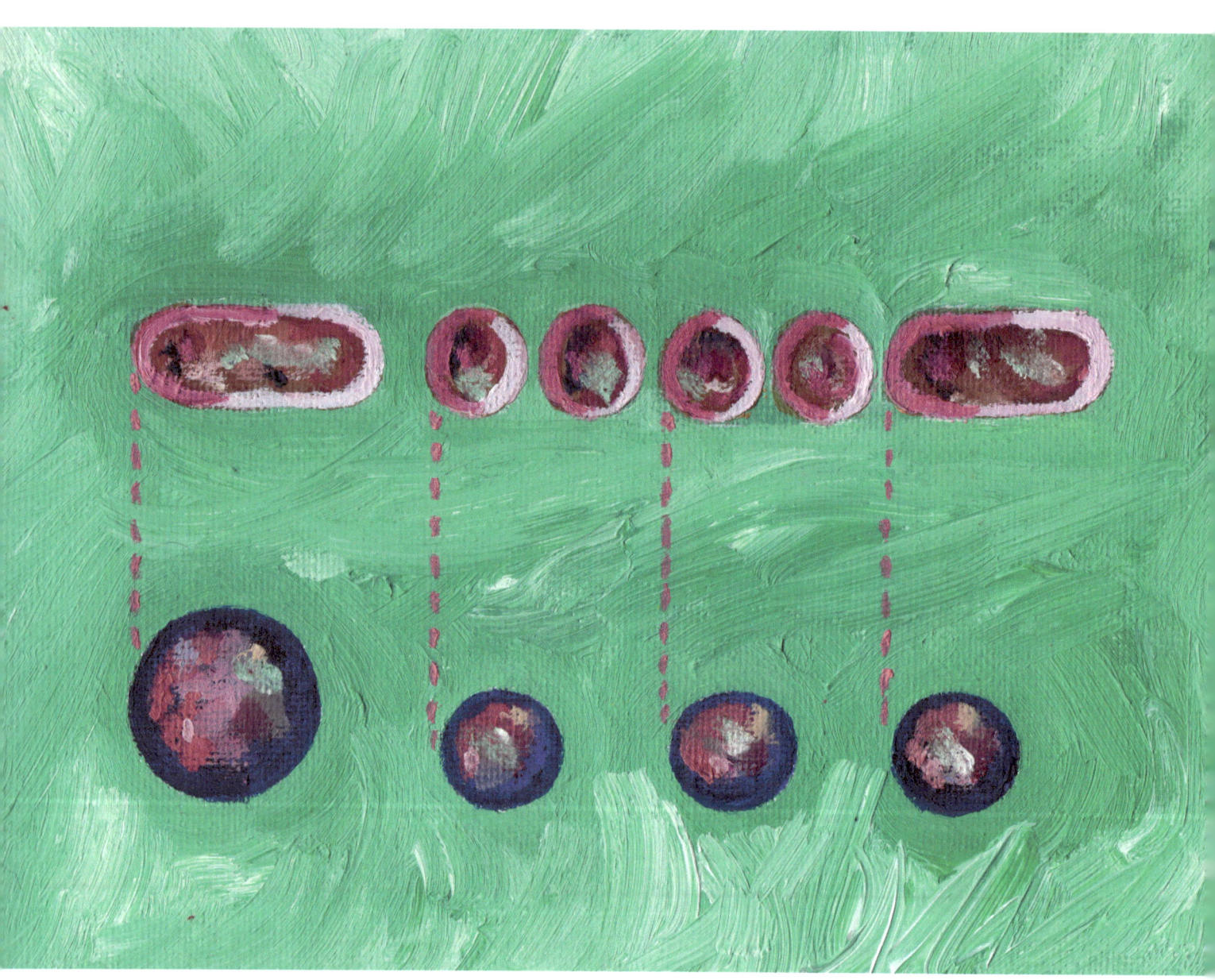

SNAP snap snap snap

Pop-py pay pay pop-py

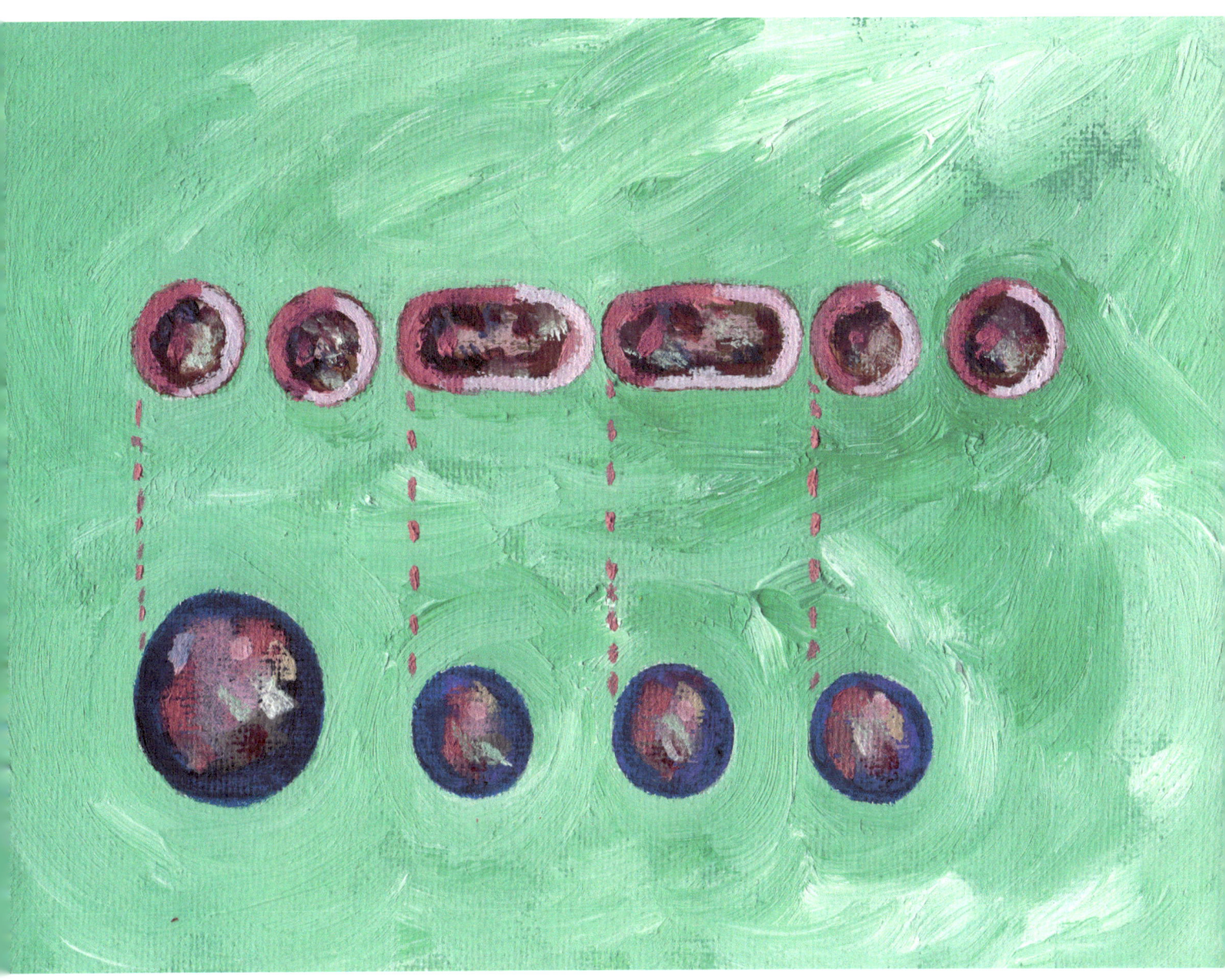

SNAP snap snap snap

Pop-py pop-py pop-py pay

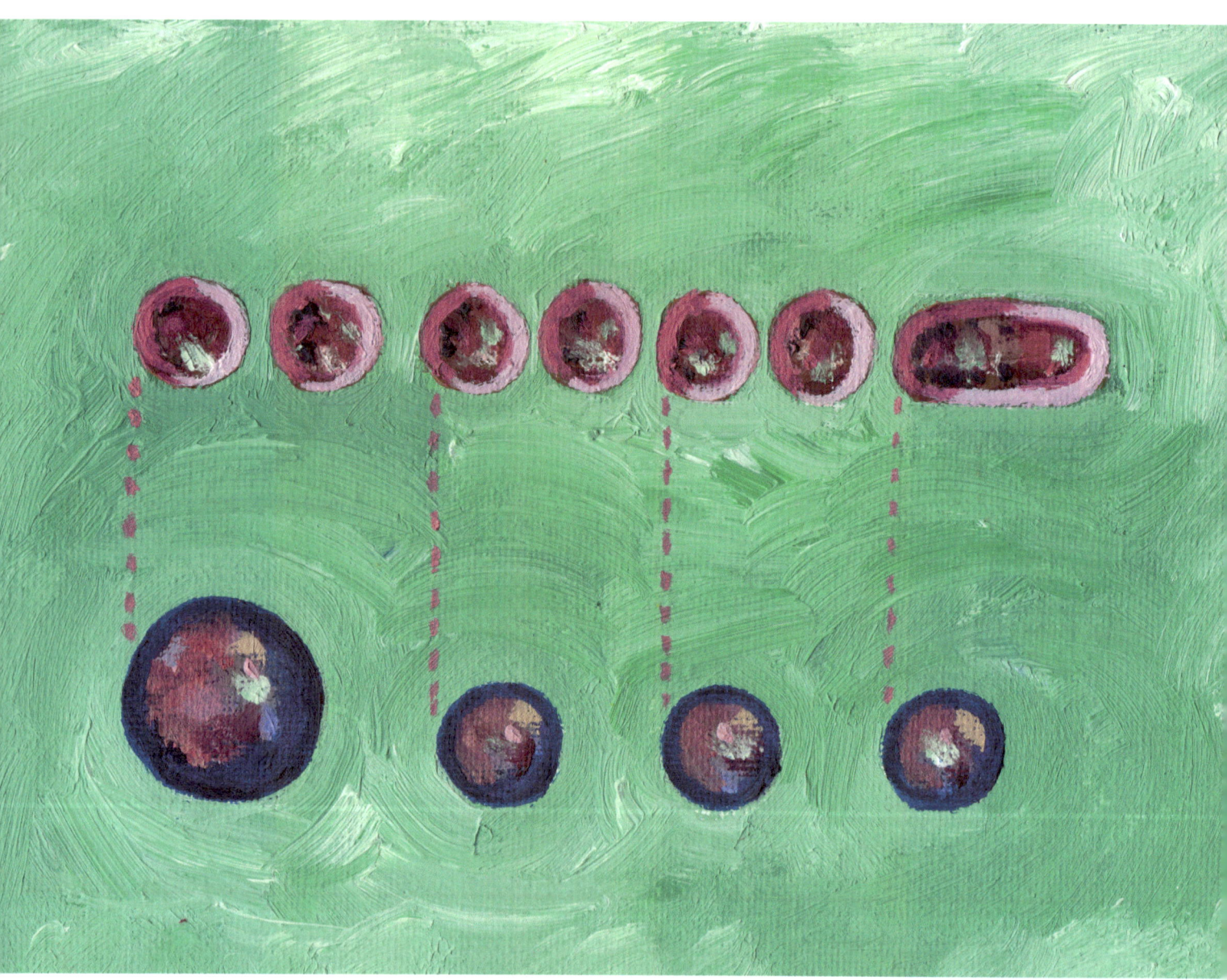

SNAP snap snap snap

Pay pop-py pop-py pay

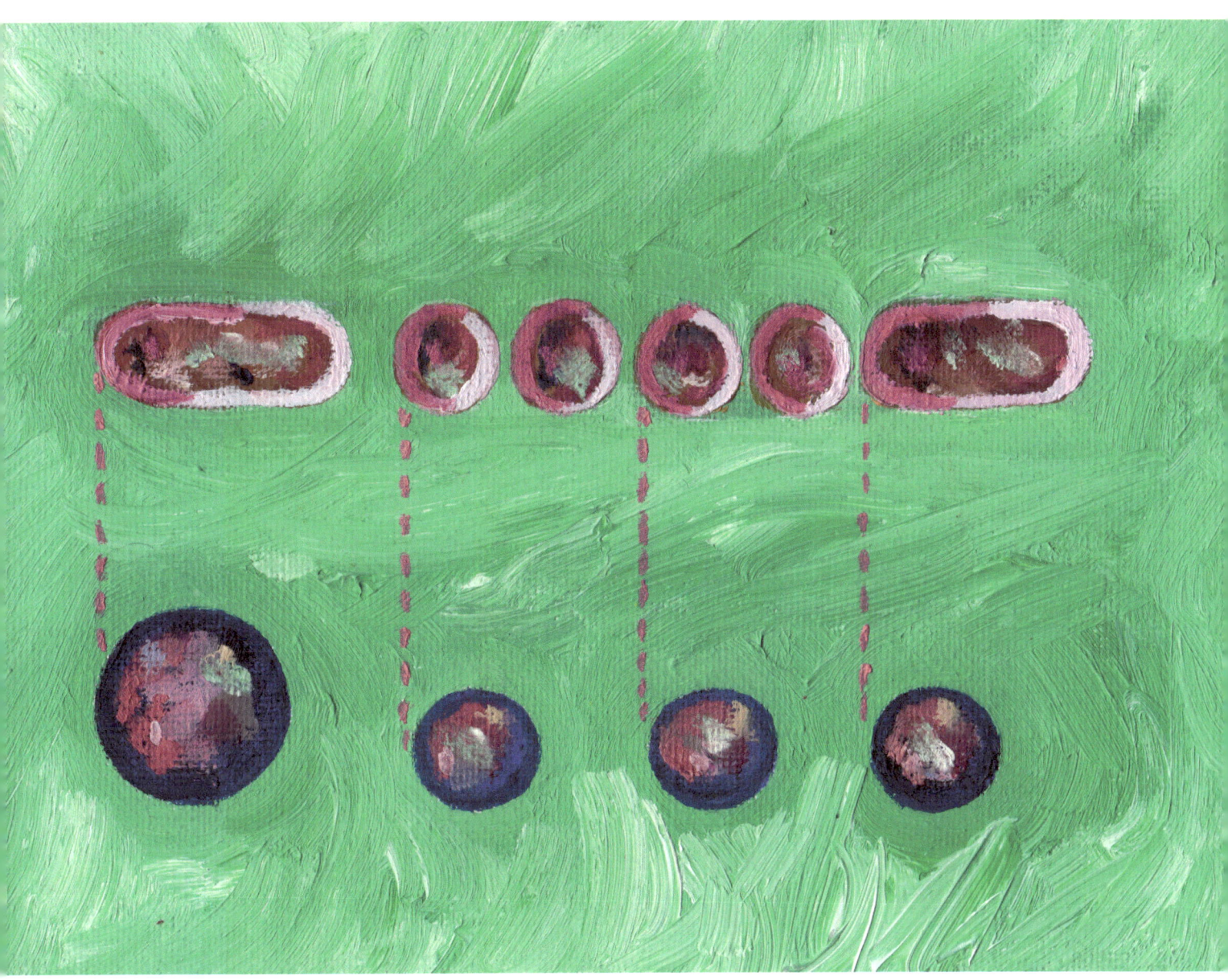

SNAP snap snap snap

Pop-py pay pay pop-py

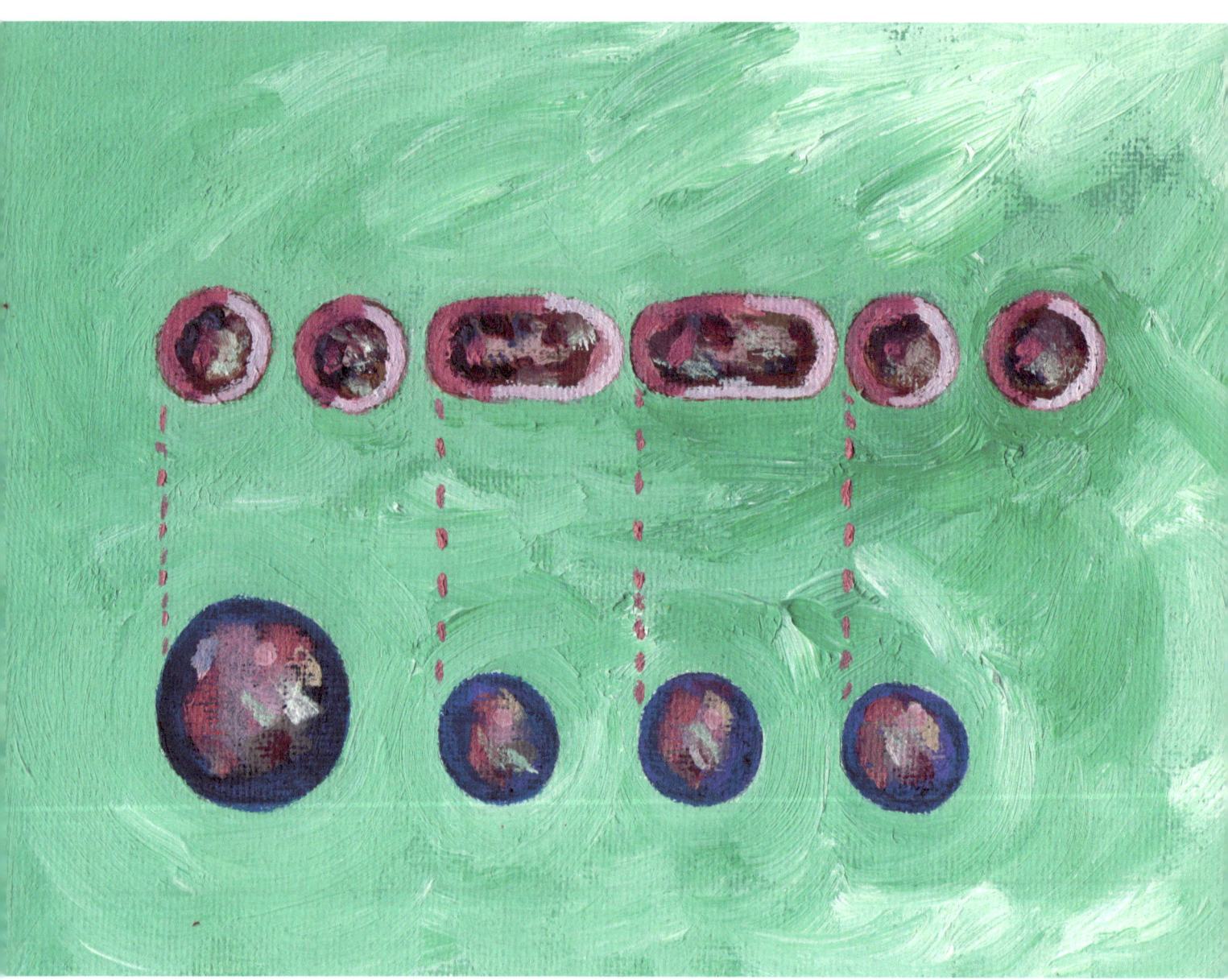

SNAP snap snap snap

156

Pop-py pop-py pay pop-py

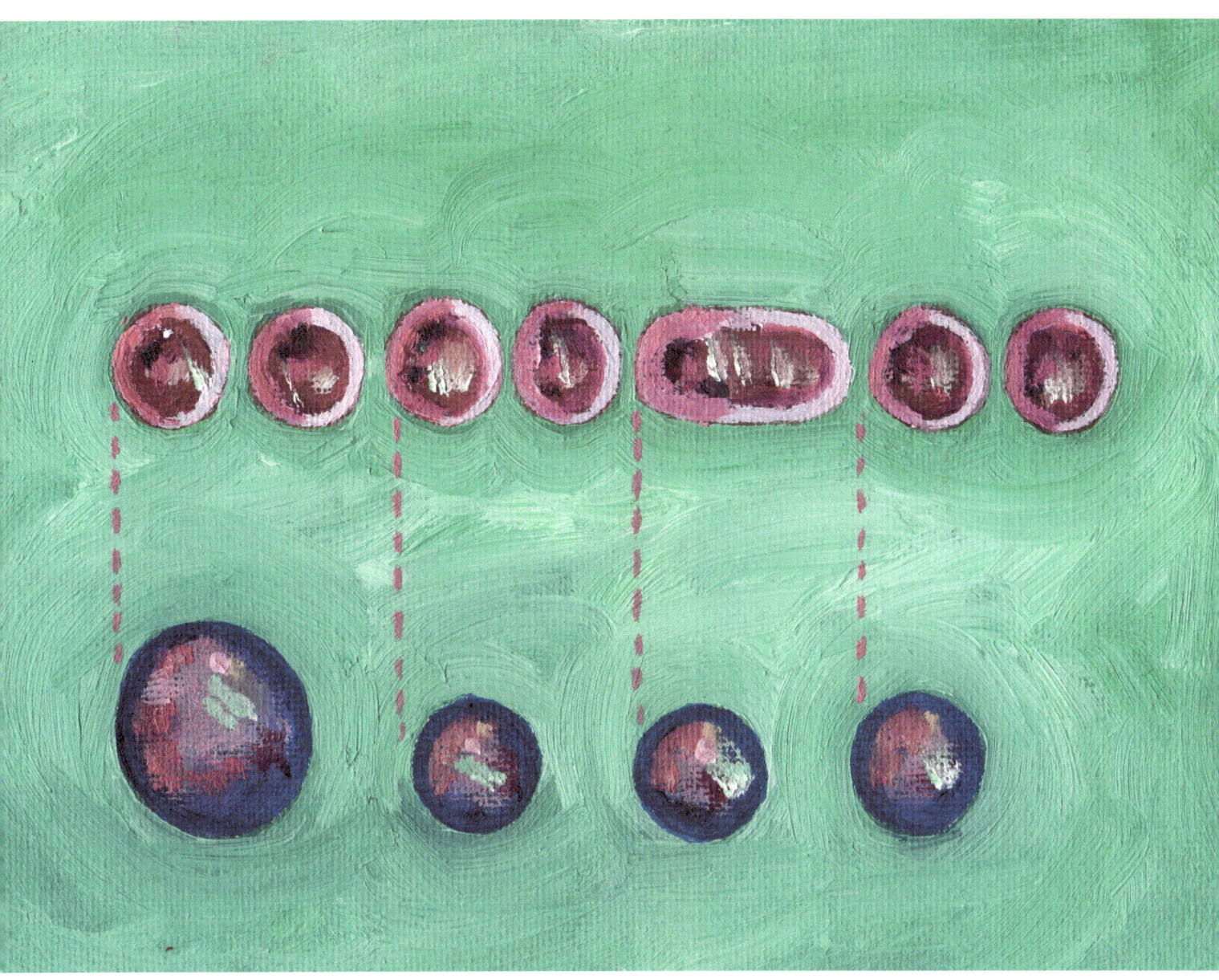

SNAP snap snap snap

CHARLENE A. RYAN is a musician, painter, writer, and mom. Across her career as a music education professor, a school music teacher, and a community music program designer, she has spent most of her life behind an instrument and in front of an audience of one kind or another.

Charlene has authored many academic papers on the performance training, experiences, and anxieties of young musicians, which has been published in leading music education and music psychology journals. She has served, and continues to serve on editorial boards for major music education journals; as editor for a national journal; and in numerous leadership roles.

Her research, teaching, and performing experiences provided the impetus for her children's books, *Hannabelle's Butterflies* and *The Milk Crate Club*, and her middle grade book, *Katherine Lost*, which center about the joys and challenges experienced by young musicians.

Her first book, Building Strong Music Programs: A Handbook for Preservice and Novice Music Teachers (NAfME/RLE) is used in teacher education programs across North America and was recognized as an Outstanding Academic Title by the Association of College and Research Libraries.

The Sound Book series developed from Charlene's work with young children and elementary students, as well as with non music-specialist university students. The books present abstract musical elements through visual art, allowing for conceptualization and actualization of complex musical concepts through straightfoward and visually appealing artwork.

Charlene is Mom to four children who educate, inspire, and sort out her technology issues on a daily basis. Together with her ever-supportive husband and two loyal labradoodles, her house and heart are full.

www.ingramcontent.com/pod-product-compliance
Lightning Source LLC
Chambersburg PA
CBHW041548120626
46551CB00002B/146